The Mountain Bike Book

The Mountain Bike Book

Choosing, riding and maintaining the
off-road bicycle

Rob Van der Plas

Bicycle Books – San Francisco

Published by:
Bicycle Books Inc.
1282a – 7th. Ave.
San Francisco, CA 94122

Distributed by:
Kampmann & Co., Inc.
9 East 40th Street
New York, NY 10016

Printed in the United States of America

Cover photograph: Stief
Frontispiece photograph: David Epperson/BICYCLE SPORT

Library of Congress Cataloging in Publication Data
Van der Plas, Robert, 1938 –
The Mountain Bike Book
Choosing, riding and maintaining the off-road bicycle
Bibliography: p. Includes index
1. Bicycles and bicycling, Manuals, Handbooks, etc.
2. Authorship – Handbooks, Manuals, etc. I. Title
Library of Congress Catalog Card Number 83-51788

ISBN 0-933201-10-9 Paperback

Table of Contents

Part I
Choosing and Using Your Mountain Bike

1
What is a Mountain Bike?

It's a lot of fun, the shortest way to inner peace, a whole new experience! Just three answers to an impossible question: a mountain bike is something different for everybody. But all who have ridden a high-quality version of the modern ATB (all terrain bike), as the mountain bike is also called, agree it is more than just a fad. Mountain bikes are here to stay, and their characteristics will leave a permanent impact on the design of all utility bicycles for the future.

Suddenly they were there: the MountainBikes, Stumpjumpers and Ridgerunners, Breezers, Trailblazers and Mount What-have-you's. Exclusive machines constructed in the workshops of meticulous craftsmen, and solidly built large-series bicycles from major manufacturers. In the span of a few years they moved from esoteric obscurity to the forefront. Today they are seriously challenging the conventional ten-speed bike built on racing lines for the status as the most popular bike in America. What is it that made these machines into such an instant success?

To describe the mountain bike in a few words, it's a light and rugged multi-speed bicycle, with very wide but light high-pressure tires, flat handlebars and reliable brakes. It differs quite significantly from all other types of bicycles in the way it handles and the abuse it will accept. It combines the forgiving robustness of the utility bike with the agility and ease of propulsion of the ten-speed.

It will go where the others get bogged down. But it will also go wherever the other bikes seemed to be in their element, except perhaps out-and-out racing on smooth roads. It's better for delivering papers than the newsboy bike, better for touring than most touring bikes, better for urban

commuting than the ten-speed, and better for just about anything than the department store special. It should be no wonder that adults who have not enjoyed riding a bike since childhood are taking to these machines, not only *buying* them (which doesn't prove much, witness the supply of bikes in any suburban garage), but also *riding* them. Mountain bikes are everything-and-everywhere-bikes!

I use the term 'mountain bike', as opposed to the many other suggested names, in a generic sense because it quite simply seems to be the most widely accepted term. Off-road bike, ATB, ballooner, fat-tire bike, cross-country touring bike are some of the other names proposed. The problem is perhaps that the term MountainBike (with two capitals and without a space) is a registered trademark, owned by one of the commercial and technical pioneers in the field. Without the capitals, and written in two words, it's the most widely used name, even though a lot of them never get close to a mountain.

A Little History

Although the mountain bike is a very recent development as such, its roots can be traced back to as early as 1933. In that year Ignaz Schwinn introduced the fat-tired bicycle in the US, that would soon become the standard for newspaper delivery, and is indeed still used for that purpose around the country today. Introduced as a sales gimmick, it emulated the design of the car with its fat tires, wide seat and high-swept handlebars, which resulted in an upright posture. These things weighed in at around 50 lbs, and the weight as well as the fat low-pressure tires offered an enormous impediment to purposeful locomotion and acceleration alike. Small wonder that the owners of such machines considered cycling an impractical and tiring mode of transportation, suitable only for the immediate neighborhood and for the fields, where Mom's car couldn't take them. And adults wouldn't dream of riding a bike.

After the Second World War some European utility bicycles started to make their entry into the United States market. Fifteen pounds lighter, and equipped with three-speed gearing, hand brakes and with narrower tires that were both lighter and allowed a higher pressure, these most plebeian of European workhorses would outsprint and outlast any utility bike in town. 'English racers' is what they would soon be dubbed – a term that makes any English cyclist's hair stand on end, but which seemed justified considering the basis for comparison.

However, it didn't take some of the big manufacturers long to ruin whatever virtue this design had: in their ceaseless effort to make things cheaper and shoddier, they dumped their wares on the unwitting customer's doorstep by way of the cheap

(James Cassimus / BICYCLE SPORT photograph)

department store market – Schwinn being perhaps the most notable exception, delivering quality and durability, albeit at a higher price and at a weight which defied comparison with the European original. Soon the English racer had degenerated to equally as inefficient (and less reliable) a machine as the old American one-speed ballooner had ever been.

Next came the ten-speed revolution. Starting in the late sixties, bicycles with derailleur gearing and skinny high-pressure tires started to invade the US. Some of these were expensive and sophisticated enough to make cycling respectable. Again it didn't take long for the major US manufacturers and importers to flood the market with wares that were so poorly constructed, so uncomfortable and so unreliable that – though these bikes were quickly sold – many would never be ridden. Just the same, bicycling as a sport and as a means of transportation was rediscovered by many adults in those years. Properly adjusted, maintained and used, the good ten-speeds could be surprisingly efficient and comfort-

able – as long as they were ridden on well surfaced roads: hardly the thing for the outback, and often not even suitable for the urban jungle, with sewer grates, chuck holes and broken bottles.

Another ingredient in the evolutionary recipe from which the modern mountain bike would eventually emerge was added in the early 70's: the BMX or 'bicycle motor cross' bicycle. Designed for kids to have fun – not for transportation – these small, light and rigid machines got kids interested in bikes, as ten-speeds had done for adults. These bikes were in their element wherever the road didn't lead: the rougher the terrain, the more fun. Their light wheels with firm wide tires combined excellent traction on any surface with responsiveness and easy acceleration and maneuverability. However, these bikes were geared so low as to be next to useless on the road, except for extremely short distances.

About the same time as the BMX bicycle made its first appearance, kids on bikes and adult motorcyclists made a sport of riding down steep hillsides, most notably on the slopes of Mount Tamalpais in Marin County, just north of San Francisco, but the same was happening elsewhere too. When the county authorities succeeded in banning motorcyclists from the Marin County trails, the men took a leaf out of the boys' book: they took to bicycles. Like the kids, they soon discovered that the old American utility bike lent itself quite well to the abuse on steep rock-strewn descents. One pickup truck was all that was needed to get half a dozen bikes and riders up the hill. At the bottom of the hill the equipment would be inspected, evaluated, discussed and repaired, replaced or discarded.

Slowly the weak parts were weeded out, and the strongest survived. Probably the most successful of all the bikes used proved to be the early Schwinn Excelsior, as it was built from 1933 until 1941. Along came bicycle racer Gary Fisher, who thought it silly to wait for a truck to get up the hill: he modified his Schwinn to take derailleur gearing and powerful handbrakes. Now you could ride up as well as down – have twice the fun. It didn't take long for another member of the crowd, frame builder Joe Breeze, to decide that the secret of the Schwinn Excelsior did not lie in its 50 or so pounds, but rather in its geometry, i.e. in the dimensions and angles to which the bike's frame had been designed. Breeze copied those dimensions to build a frame that weighed a lot less, equipped it with suitable components, and the mountain bike was born... except, they forgot to shout "Eureka" and tell the world, so the world had to wait a few more year to find out about it.

Meanwhile, the men in California and Colorado continued to have their fun; some even combined it with business. Several frame builders took up the art of perfecting the mountain bike to minimize its weight, while improving its handling characteristics and its reliability. Others sought out components to perfect the whole: aluminum alloy rims with matching tires that would take the pressure to provide maximum cushioning and good traction as well as low rolling resistance, strong and reliable brakes, dust proof and water resistant bearings, wide-range gearing. Whatever they didn't find, they made themselves, like the flat handlebar and stem combinations and the reinforced forks used on many bikes.

These bikes weren't cheap, and many an off-road cyclist found he could save himself the expense of a conventional machine in addition to his pride and joy of a mountain bike. There is a rumor some even had to sell their pickups, which left them with an expensive fat-tired bike as their only wheels. Not only did they ride their mountain bikes to the trail head, they also rode them to the supermarket, the massage parlor and the health food store; in fact, anywhere within cycling range. Ten-speeds were hot items, but in these early days of bicycle ballooning the mountain bikes looked too odd to attract bike thieves. Unfortunately, that has changed since those days, but the fact that these bikes proved to be surprisingly efficient and reliable on asphalt as well as on dirt was not lost on keen observers. Soon demand for these machines far exceeded the limited supply that could be handled by the local craftsmen. Time for another hero to appear.

Next on the scene was a young bicycle-businessman from San Jose, California, Mike Sinyard, the enterprising proprietor of a company called Specialized. Sinyard always had a good nose for new and interesting products, not offered competitively by others. He hired mountain bike frame builder Tim Neenan to design a suitable frame that could be produced in series, contracted for the manufacture of the frame in Japan, and equipped it with a selection of suitable components from three continents. He poured on the money in an advertising campaign that went well beyond anything ever done before on behalf of any single new model. Thus the Stumpjumper, as Sinyard called the bike, was born and rose to quick fame. It probably handsomely repaid the initial investment. Two years later Specialized returned with a slightly simpler and lower-priced model, which might have become as much a success as the Stumpjumper was.

However, the big manufacturers were close on his heels. By early 1983 several of the major Japanese manufacturers and a number of domestic suppliers boasted series-production mountain bikes. The manufacturers now began to get the wind of real big bucks. Several companies contracted with experienced mountain bike frame builders, not only to do what Sinyard had done first, but also to build some exclusive bikes for limited sale to the public and for the use by sponsored racers on the company's team. References like Murray and Ross started to appear behind the names of successful participants in off-road races, sharing the honors with men riding equipment which bear the names of the handful of California and Colorado frame builders, who mostly remained in the less enviable position of having to *sell* the bike to the rider in order to make a living.

By now it was early spring 1983. The bicycle trade publications reported that 10 % of all adult bike sales were in the category of moun-

tain bikes, with an increasing proportion of that going to the major manufacturers. Not that the specialty frame builders were starving: racers and discriminating or well-heeled riders were still opting for their products, and willing to pay the price. But at the same time prices of production mountain bikes declined rapidly, without quite such a lowering of the technical standards as had been experienced before during the ten-speed boom. It seems mountain bike customers are more critical buyers, who are prepared to pay a little more to get quality, even if they may never use their full potential.

Mountain bike pioneer Tom Ritchey on one of his MountainBikes. (David Epperson / Bicycle Sport photograph)

(David Epperson / Bicycle Sport photograph)

The rapid growth of the mountain bike scene may perhaps be adequately illustrated by tracing the progress of that unique magazine, *Fat-Tire Flyer,* which Charles Kelly and Denise Caramagno kept alive and growing through the early years. First published in 1980 in the form of a couple of mimeographed 8½ x 11 sheets, folded in the middle and filled by the editors under various pseudonyms, it progressed to 16 pages of newsprint from typewritten copy by early 1982. One year later it was transformed into a 24 page glossy magazine with photographs and ads to match the paper quality.

No, this history of the mountain bike is not exhaustive. I haven't even begun to tell you about the sub-culture which developed around the people who build and ride these unique bikes. You haven't heard of the ride organizers, like Victor Vicente of America (don't forget the 'of America' bit) or Glenn Odell, who put the off-road cycling association NORBA on a commercial footing. I haven't said a word about the fine women riders, like Jacquie Phelan, Denise Caramagno and Wende Cragg. There are a hundred other names, facts and figures left out of this account. Some of these gaps will be filled in as the book progresses, many others should perhaps wait until somebody writes a compendium of fat-tire anecdotes. For the time being, I feel this is as much history as is fit to print: let's return to the present.

2
A Close Look at the Mountain Bike

There are at least two different ways of looking at a mountain bike: as a novice or as a cyclist. What you see is the same, but what you'll notice most may differ. I'll try to satisfy both categories of readers as much as possible. For the edification of either group, I'll highlight the differences between the mountain bike and the conventional ten-speed. That will help the experienced cyclist understand the mountain bike in terms of the differences and similarities relative to his earlier machines, while it will help the novice to not only get familiar with the mountain bike, but also learn a little about bicycles and bicycling in general.

The illustrations below and overleaf show typical representatives of the two varieties: a mountain bike and a ten-speed 'racing' bike. I put the quotation marks around 'racing' on purpose, since most of these bikes would be totally out of place in any bicycle race, though they look to

all the world just like the real thing. On the other hand, 'ten-speed' isn't a very useful term either, since a number of cheap mountain bikes come equipped with the same ten gears. Perhaps the fairest terminology would be the one used by Charles Kelly and other members of the competetive off-road scene: they distinguish between *Fat-Tire Bikes* (preferably with all those capitals) and *skinny tire bikes* (hold the capitals).

The drawing of the mountain bike is fully captioned with the names of all the bits and pieces that make up the bicycle. In the picture of the skinny tire bike, only the significant visible differences are pointed out. The major components themselves each comprise quite a few separate parts (up to about 500, as is the case with the chain). But the easiest way to look at the bike and its components is by grouping the latter into several major categories: frame, steering system, wheels, drive-train,

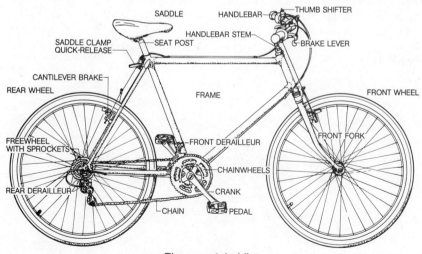

The mountain bike

gearing, brakes, saddle and accessories. In the chapters 10 through 18 of Part II of this book, the technical details of all the major parts will be described for each component group. At this point I'll merely introduce each of these complexes, describing them in rough outline, and pointing out the most significant differences between the mountain bike and the conventional ten-speed bicycle. The same remarks help you distinguish between a good mountain bike and a poor one, as inadequate models will inevitably hit the market about the same time as this book: there'll never be a good idea, that can not be perverted by the objectionable business mentality of making it cheaper and shoddier.

The Frame

As on any other bicycle, the mountain bike's frame forms the backbone of the entire machine. Usually it is the only part actually made by the manufacturer whose name and logo appear on the frame; all other components are bought from specialized suppliers and fitted to the finished frame. Final assembly is done in the factory or, in the case of some custom-built bikes, in the bike shop. The frame is almost always constructed of round tubular steel, which may be either welded or brazed together at the joints.

The frame consists of the quadrilateral main frame, built with large-diameter tubing, and a double rear triangle of smaller diameter tubing. The main frame comprises the short and stubby head tube, in which the steering system is pivoted, the horizontal (or nearly horizontal) top tube, the nearly vertical seat tube, and the slanting down tube, which connects the lower ends of the head and seat tubes. A short tube, called bottom bracket shell, runs perpendicular to the other tubes, and forms the connecting link between the main frame and the lower portion of the rear triangle. This bottom bracket is the heart of the bicycle's drive-train, housing the bearings for the cranks.

The rear triangle consists of the seat stays, which run from the rear wheel axle to the top of the seat tube, and the chain stays, running from the

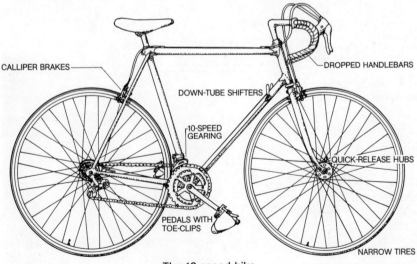

CALLIPER BRAKES

DROPPED HANDLEBARS

DOWN-TUBE SHIFTERS

10-SPEED GEARING

QUICK-RELEASE HUBS

PEDALS WITH TOE-CLIPS

NARROW TIRES

The 10-speed bike

rear wheel axle to the bottom bracket. The pairs of stays are each connected by short tubular bridges. Though the front triangle differs little from that of a conventional bicycle, except that usually slightly larger diameter tubing with a heavier wall thickness is used, the rear triangle should be designed differently. To clear the thicker tires of the mountain bike, the chain stays are usually not straight, as on the conventional bike, but 'dog-legged'. In addition, the seat stays usually have bosses welded or brazed on, to take the so-called cantilever brakes, used on most mountain bikes.

Another difference is most clearly seen on the assembled bike: the total length of the frame and the clearances between the wheels and the frame are usually considerably greater on the mountain bike than they are on the regular ten-speed. This not only gives the clearances to keep the wheels rolling in thick mud, it also keeps the rider's weight safely centered between the wheels, even when cycling up or down a steep slope.

The Steering System

Believe it or not, bicycles are not steered by just turning the handlebars one way or the other, but by judiciously leaning the bike in the direction of the turn. Even going straight involves constant corrections in the amount of lean. The steering system follows the lean of the bike to provide the right curve: that's what makes it possible to ride hands-off. But under off-road conditions the unevennesses in the surface will disturb this self-guiding principle. So expect to be 'fighting' the handlebars a lot more on rough ground than on the road.

The components of the steering system are the handlebars, the front fork and the head-set bearings, which are mounted in the frame's head tube. Technical details will be treated in chapter 12, *The Steering System,* but here are the differences relative to the skinny-tire bike. The handlebars are flat, for an upright riding posture, and wide, for more leverage under off-road conditions. The stem, which connects the handlebars to the fork, must be stronger and must hold the handlebars tighter, to accept the greater forces applied to it. The fork should be stronger, especially near the top, and the clearance between the blades of the fork must be big enough for the fatter tires. In addition, there will usually be bosses for installation of the brakes attached to the front of the fork blades. Like the frame, the fork will usually be enamel-coated in black, grey, olive or some other such earthy hue.

The Wheels

Ever since John Boyd Dunlop introduced the pneumatic tire in the year 1887, the wheels have formed the bicycle's major suspension system. At least 90 % of this is attributable to cushioning of the air-filled tires, the

Front end of high-quality series bike (John Kirkpatrick / Ross Bicycles photograph)

Well-designed mass-production mountain bike (photo: Raleigh Corporation of America)

rest to flexing of the spoked wheel and the front fork. Each wheel consists of a central hub with ball bearings, a set of usually 36 wire spokes, a metal rim, an inner tube and a tire cover. The construction is the same for a mountain bike as for any other bicycle – except for the dimensions and the resulting cushioning effect.

On a racing bike, the tire has an outside diameter of about 685 mm (27 in) and a cross section of about 25 mm (1 in). That results in an air chamber containing about 1 liter (approx. 65 cu in). On a mountain bike, that air chamber has nearly the same outside diameter, namely 660 mm (26 in). But the cross section is about twice as big, namely 47 mm to 57 mm, depending on the nominal tire size (1.75 to 2.125 in). This provides an air chamber with on average four times the volume, resulting in four times the cushioning effect. Although it had been long believed that thicker tires have a higher rolling resistance, experience and experiment have shown that this is not so:

as long as the fat tire is inflated to the same high pressure, the rolling resistance is similar to that of a narrower tire. Modern fat tires differ from old-fashioned balloon tires in that they allow the high air pressures which result in low rolling resistance.

The rims are another vital element in this relationship. They must hold the tire at the high inflation pressure, and they should be as light as possible. For this reason, and to provide good braking when wet, all respectable mountain bikes have aluminum rims. Those rims are of a different size than the conventional rims used for ten-speeds: smaller in diameter and quite a bit wider. The other parts of the wheel – spokes and the hub – are similar to those used on high-quality ten-speeds, though stronger versions should be used, and usually the hubs are not held in the frame and the fork by means of a quick-release mechanism, as they are on most ten-speeds of comparable quality, but by means of nuts, screwed straight onto the axle.

Drive-Train and Gearing

Like the ten-speed, essentially all mountain bikes use derailleur gearing. Together with the drive-train proper, consisting of cranks, pedals, bottom bracket, chain, chainwheels and freewheel, the derailleurs must be judiciously selected on any bicycle. On the mountain bike, certain components that were developed for the conventional ten-speed touring bike have proven themselves, while other components were either borrowed from BMX-technology or are specifically made for this kind of machine.

To describe the whole system briefly, the rider's output is transmitted from the pedals, over the levers formed by the cranks to the chainwheels, which rotate around the bottom bracket bearings. The chain takes the power from there to the sprockets (i.e. small chainwheels) which are connected by means of a freewheel mechanism to the rear hub, driving the rear wheel. The derailleurs quite literally 'derail' the chain, placing it on one of several possible combinations of differently sized chainwheels and sprockets, as controlled from levers, which on the mountain bike are always mounted within easy reach on the flat handlebars.

Mountain bikes usually are equipped with fifteen or eighteen speeds: three chainwheels up front and five or six sprockets in the back. The crankset of any respectable mountain bike is of a cotterless construction, as it is on conventional ten-speeds of comparable quality. The length of the cranks is often somewhat bigger than it is on regular bikes, and the range of gearing is wider. To ride uphill you will need very low gears, which are provided by a very small third chainwheel in the front, and a freewheel with sprockets that may have anywhere from 26 to 34 teeth as the biggest. Naturally the derailleurs must be selected to match this choice of gears.

The pedals installed on mountain bikes do not have the toe-clips, generally used on racing bikes. Usually they are very big and have vicious looking teeth, to provide a firm hold for the feet. Quite often on quality mountain bikes, special sealed bearings are used on pedals, hubs and crankset. There are even derailleurs which are sealed to minimize the penetration of moisture and dirt, which would interfere with the smooth operation when the bike is used in wet or dirty conditions.

The Brakes

Mountain bikes need brakes more than any other kind of bicycle. That's why the most powerful and reliable brakes are selected for such machines. Almost without exception cantilever brakes are used, mounted directly to the frame (in the rear) and the front fork (in the front). This is

Fifteen-speed gearing means tripple chainwheels in the front.

another difference that sets the mountain bike apart from most conventional ten-speed bicycles, which are generally equipped with calliper brakes. The latter work fine on bikes with small cross-section tires, but are inadequate if made in a size to fit around the enormously fat tires used on the mountain bike.

Brakes are controlled from hand-operated levers, mounted close to the ends of the flat handlebars. These levers must be of a different design from those meant for dropped handlebars, to match the contour of the handlebars, and to be within the rider's reach. Often motorcycle levers are used; similarly it is a good idea to install the thicker control cables made for motorcycle use. Such cables are less susceptible to stretch, thus eliminating the 'spungy' feel of many bicycle braking systems.

Saddle and Seatpost
Even in these details mountain bikes are often different. To allow for changes in saddle height and forward position, often required to adapt to a change in the terrain, the mountain bike comes with a more easily adjusted saddle. The saddle itself should be somewhat wider than that found on a racing bike, to offer reasonable comfort in the upright position. The saddle is connected to the frame's seat tube by means of a seat post, which is held in the frame by means of a clamp. On mountain bikes this clamp is equipped with a quick-release mechanism. The seat post should be quite long to allow plenty of adjustment, since the frame for a mountain bike should be selected several inches smaller than that of a regular bike for the same size rider.

Accessories
Sensible accessories just aren't a big thing on any kind of bicycle sold in the US, and the mountain bike is no exception. Due to an obscure and unscientific Consumer Product Safety Commission ruling, all bicycles sold must be equipped with a plethora of ill-conceived reflectors on the wheels, the pedals, behind the seat and in the front. You needn't keep them on the bike, though: the law applies to the point of sale, not to the equipment used when riding. But install a light in the front and a big reflector in the back if you ride your bike in traffic at night.

Other things that seem to be inevitable on any bicycle sold in most other countries, but are always left off American bikes, are fenders and luggage racks. There is not a mountain bike on the market today that is equipped with fenders. In fact, fenders are hard to find even as accessories, so the mud will flie around your ears, unless you install your own. It's a different story with luggage racks: most mountain bikes come equipped with special attachment lugs for luggage racks. Several manufacturers of racks make special models for

Quick chain lubrication with the spray can

mountain bikes, both for the front and for the rear. There are even special bags, intended for mountain bike use, taking full advantage of the more generous dimensions of the mountain bike, and usually made of sturdier materials than are used for regular bicycle luggage.

Care of the Mountain Bike

Mountain bikes are meant to get dirty. However, to get optimal performance and life expectancy, your machine should be cleaned and lubricated as soon as possible once you get it dirty. Don't wait until you're ready for the next ride, but do it right away when you get back home. If the dirt is wet, wash it off with plenty of water, a scrubbing brush and a rag. Get into every nook and cranny, including such hard-to-reach places as the gaps between the sprockets and the inside of derailleur mechanisms and brakes. Wipe everything dry as soon as you've finished. If the dirt is dry, first brush as much off as possible before you go to it with the water-and-brush treatment.

After this cleaning operation some parts of the bike are easy prey to corrosion, since lubricants and protective grease may have been removed while washing and scrubbing. As a very minimum, get yourself a spray can of thin-flowing lubricant, such as WD-40 or the lightest version of LPS. Aim the tube which fits on the nozzle at all the bare-metal parts that might need lubrication and protection, i.e. every mechanism, pivot, joint, bolt,

Main lubrication points of the bicycle: Clean and relubricate frequently.

nut and quick-release, the cables and their levers, the chain with its chainwheels and sprockets. Don't get it on the sides of the rims (since you'd ruin the brakes' effectiveness) and the parts you will be touching when operating the gears and the brakes. Wipe off excess superficial lubricants.

When you get more ambitious about bicycle care, you are advised to refer to the specific maintenance recommendations in the chapters of Part II of this book. There you will learn which lubricants are the most appropriate for which purposes, how to make adjustments, overhauls and repairs, as well as how to establish what needs to be done if your bike is not performing as it should. Even if you are not at all technically ambitious, get yourself a screwdriver and a small adjustable wrench, and use them to check and tighten every bolt, nut and screw on the bike from time to time. Whenever you find something to be amiss, either get it fixed by the bike shop right away, or find out in Part II of the book how to do it yourself.

3
Selecting a Mountain Bike

As this book goes to press, nearly two dozen major manufacturers and at least as many specialist builders offer mountain bikes, ranging in price from around $250 to well over $2000. Despite previous experience with inflation, which made the hundred-dollar bike of 1974 cost $ 250 ten years later, I feel these prices may well remain intact for quite a few years. With increased competition for a share of the big mountain-bike pie, prices of mass-produced machines are not going to climb. In

(David Epperson / BICYCLE SPORT photograph)

fact, lower-priced machines will almost certainly come on the market; but these can only be cheaper than the present minimum of about $ 250 by being significantly less sophisticated: inferiorly constructed and inadequately equipped.

At the high end of the scale, there is not much chance of a lowering of prices, though increased competition is not likely to allow an increase either. The price of such individually designed and constructed machines is not determined by market forces, but simply by the number of hours of work that goes into their construction, and to a lesser extent by the price of the equipment installed. Neither of these two factors is likely to change significantly enough to warrant a dramatic reduction in price.

What may happen, though, is the introduction of large-series machines, built to satisfy the most demanding riders, at prices that are much lower than those the specialized frame builder has to charge. Even so, there will always be a market for the exclusive products of these frame builders, just like there always is a market for hand-knotted oriental rugs, even in the age of cheap wall-to-wall shag carpeting.

So much for the range of prices. Now, how do you go about choosing the right bike for your use? Before I get any further into this subject matter, let me give you three absolute 'don'ts':

1. Never buy any bike, whether a mountain bike or any other type, anywhere except at a bicycle shop.

2. Don't buy an 'unbranded' bike, a machine no manufacturer acknowledges as his product, and largely

Top-of-the line series machine (John Kirkpatrick / Ross Bicycles photograph)

equipped with similarly unbranded components.

3. Never buy any bike right away: take the time to look at some more models, sleep over it, and take your time making up your mind. Don't be rushed, even if the salesperson tells you this is a unique opportunity to get a better bike at a lower price.

The Right Size

The most expensive and sophisticated bicycle is not going to be safe and comfortable if it's the wrong size. You're better off with a simple bike that fits than with a fancy one that doesn't. That applies to other bicycles too, but it is even more important for a mountain bike, on which more complicated maneuvers are made. Conventional bike sizing guidelines can not be used to establish the correct size of a mountain bike. That's because several things are different:

1. Mountain bikes are often measured by a different method than regular bikes.

2. One of the sizing reference points, the bottom bracket, is usually

higher on a mountain bike than it is on most other machines.

3. On a mountain bike you must be able to adust the saddle up and down over a longer range than on a regular bike.

The illustration shows how the frame size of a mountain bike is commonly measured, as compared to the method of measuring other bicycle frames. Some manufacturers measure the same way, i.e. center of bottom bracket to top of seat lug; so make sure you know which dimension is being quoted: deduct the distance from the center of the top tube to the top of the seat lug (usually about ¾ to 1 in) from the seat-tube length to get the correct center-to-center dimension. The correct

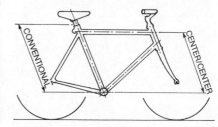

frame size is a function of the rider's leg length; you must be able to straddle the frame with both feet flat on the ground. Rules of thumb based on the rider's total body height are totally useless, since two persons with the same height may well have quite different leg lengths. You may use Table 3-I as a rough guide to the required frame size, keeping in mind that it is safer to deviate on the low side than on the high side.

This is just the beginning: you have determined what might be *about* the right size, but you haven't finished yet. A bike that fits is a bike that can be ridden comfortably, and there is more to riding a bike than reaching the pedals. You will have to actually try sitting on a bike before you can be sure to have found the right size. The second most important dimension is the distance between the seat and the handlebars. On ten-speed bikes this dimension is varied primarily by means of installing a longer or shorter handlebar extension or stem. Since those flat handlebars installed on mountain bikes either have an integral stem or come with a special stem of a fixed size, you won't be able to make this adjustment on a ready-made mountain bike.

Sit on a bike set up in the shop, after having adjusted the saddle for normal riding in accordance with the illustration. Pedal backward to check whether this position is indeed comfortable, making sure you have the front of the foot (neither the heel, nor the arch of the foot) on the pedal.

Table 3-I Recommended frame sizes for mountain bikes

Leg length*	maximum recommended frame size**
29	17
30	18
31	19
32	19
33	20
34	21
35	22
36	22

* measured per R.H. detail
** measured per L.H. detail
all dimensions in inches

Now check the position of the handlebars. Get them moved up or down until they are level with the top of the saddle. In this position you should be comfortable and relaxed, your trunk and arms being inclined approximately as shown in the illustration. If your arms, your hands or your shoulders are obviously straining, the distance between the saddle and the handlebars is probably too great. If you feel the desire to stretch out further, they are probably too close together.

The latter evil can not easily be corrected without sacrificing other, more desirable, features. So if you can't get used to it, you will have to get an expensive custom-made stem. The former problem, seat and handlebars too far apart, may often be corrected by trying a smaller frame. The trick is that most manufacturers make the top tube on bigger bikes longer than they do on

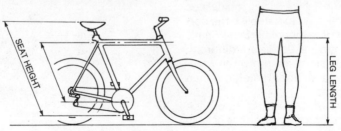

SEAT HEIGHT

LEG LENGTH

smaller bikes. As the frame size goes from 17 in to 23 in, the top tube length may increase from 22 in to 25 in. Try a slightly smaller frame, and see whether you are more comfortable. If not, try a different make of bike, since different manufacturers may well use slightly different proportions.

Some minor correction may also be made by adjusting the saddle back or forth. However, I suggest you keep the center of the saddle close to the center of the seat post in the 'relaxed' position, so you leave some adjustment range to accommodate to changes in the terrain encountered. Climbing you may want your saddle further forward; going down you will want to move it back a little. Don't despair if this sounds very tricky: at least 95 % of all cyclists can find a comfortable stock bicycle to fit them, even though it may take some trial and error – another good reason not to buy on impulse.

Riding posture

Kinds of Mountain Bikes

Even within the narrow category of mountain bikes, and as early as this is in the development of the off-road bicycle, several distinct categories can be recognized. As with tenspeed bikes, one may distinguish between light and heavy, mass-produced and custom-built, well-equipped and mediocre. But there is also another distinction which seems to cut through these conventional demarcations. To give them names, I will stick out my neck at this point and distinguish between three categories:

1. True off-road bicycles, ultimately suitable to go where the paved road doesn't, and equipped with the fattest, grippiest 26 x 2.125 tires.

2. Mixed use mountain bikes, quite suitable for unpaved trails and on any pavement, equipped with the somewhat lighter 26 x 1.75 tires.

3. Fat-tire touring bikes, which will take on almost any kind of pavement and will not get stuck immediately on unpaved roads, equipped with the French tire size 650 x 35B.

Seat height

Before you dismiss any one of these models, consider what kind of use you will give your bike. Though the heavy, knobby 26 x 2.125 tires of the true off-road machine sound very impressive on smooth pavement, they are heavier and they offer both higher rolling resistance and slower acceleration. I will discuss these matters more fully in the chapter devoted to the wheels, and it is possible to change wheels from a thicker to a slimmer type (though not always the other way round). But there is no point buying equipment you do not need: each bike offers the best combination of characteristics in its intended environment. It is not merely the wheel size that differs: there are other differences too, but the wheel size is usually the giveaway.

To give you an idea of my own preferences, I have two mountain bikes in my household. One of these is on a long-term loan from a framebuilder, whom I feed with suggestions for modifications and technical solutions of other problems in return for an ever further extended loan period. This machine is a true-to-life off-road bicycle, which I use for exactly that purpose. The other machine is what I call a mixed-use mountain bike. It gets a lot of use on poorly paved roads and whenever I have to ride in inclement weather. I have frequently ridden it on snow and ice, where it actually performs better than the true off-road bike, which seems to build snow balls around the knobby tires. For long-distance work and any riding on good roads I use one of my skinny-tired ten-speeds, which definitely have their advantages under such circumstances.

Of course, road surface quality is probably the most significant factor that should affect the choice of machine. Two Englishmen crossed the Sahara on American-built true off-road mountain bikes. I have reports from quite a few folks who have done the same on all kinds of other bicycles, and I have heard of all sorts of mechanical problems – ranging from 16 flats a day to broken frames. The two English mountain

Pseudo mountain bike: fine for urban cycling, but not for real off-road use (photo: Raleigh Corporation of America).

bike riders completed the roughest stretch from Algiers to Lagos without any mechanical breakdown: no flat, no broken spoke, no bent crank and a frame that stayed in one piece. But... just in case you are not going to cross the Sahara, choose the appropriate equipment to save money and to maximize the enjoyment you get from cycling.

Custom-Made or Factory-Built?

All custom-built bikes are quite a bit more expensive than series machines. That even holds true for bikes which are otherwise quite similar in quality. But the highest quality machines and those that are truly optimized to the rider's needs, certainly if those needs are at all of a competitive nature, quite simply *have* to be custom-built. Don't be fooled by the factory logos on some of the machines used in off-road races by factory teams, such as Raleigh, Murray or Ross. Such bikes are not the mass-production models made by those manufacturers: they are custom-built, just like those of other participants. That is a trend copied from European road racing, where teams sponsored by large manufacturers ride bikes with that company's logo on it, that being the only thing those bikes have in common with most regular machines made by the same company.

However, if you don't participate in off-road races and don't aspire to do all the masterful tricks that are performed there, you will probably be well served with almost any mass-produced bike of respectable quality. I even think some of the competitive off-road racers could probably run the pants off just about anybody else, and might well do as well in some races, on a factory-built bike. In the chapters about the frame and the steering mechanism I will explain some of the differences between various designs. At this point it should suffice to say that most major manufacturers offer well-balanced designs to satisfy the greatest common denominator of users and uses, at a price that is close to optimal. To get a bike that is better for one person or for one particular application, you will have to get a custom design; but that same design will not necessarily be better for another rider or for another application.

Twice the fun. Off-road tandem built by Jeff Lindsay of Mountain Goat Cycles. Even for cycling on the road this would be an excellent choice amongst tandem bicycles.

Minimum Requirements

Let me conclude this chapter with a list of items which I consider to be essential on any mountain bike. As recently as the spring of 1983 such a list would have been superfluous: anything sold as a mountain bike would satisfy all of these criteria. But as more manufacturers are getting on the bandwagon, and as new, cheaper models are introduced in an effort to offer something for everybody, things (and I mean *things*) are being sold which don't deserve the name 'mountain bike'. Watch out for the following points, to assure what you get doesn't just *look* like one, but actually *is* a real mountain bike:

1. Wheels must have aluminum rims (steel rims are too heavy, and do not provide adequate friction when braking in wet weather).

2. Cranks should be of the cotterless variety, and the right-hand crank should form one piece with the attachment spider for the chain-wheels (cottered cranks will come loose, swaged crank-and-chainwheel assemblies will bend).

3. Mountainous or other steep terrain requires fifteen- or eighteen-speed derailleur gearing, although a simpler gearing system may be adequate in relatively level areas.

4. Brakes must be either of the cantilever type, which pivot around mounting bosses permanently attached to the forks and seat stays, or special (and much more expensive) designs specifically made for off-road bicycles (ordinary calliper brakes are too flexible, coaster brakes will overheat on a long descent).

There is of course much more to be said about selecting a mountain bike than could be covered in this chapter. Consider this a summary introduction, and keep reading: the finer points which should affect your choice will all be covered in the subsequent chapters of the book.

4
Bicycle Safety On and Off the Road

You've bought your mountain bike; you're ready to go out and ride it. But before you do, let me ask you to bear with me one more chapter: your life could depend on it. Bicycle safety is an issue of major concern to public authorities and medical specialists – as it should be to the bicyclist himself. Unfortunately, a lot of false information has been put out on this subject, and the danger is very real that you are going to subject yourself to significant and unnecessary risks, exactly because you try to avoid *perceived* dangers, which everybody has warned you about.

Don't think that motor traffic is the only source of danger to the bicyclist, and that consequently the mountain bike rider is quite safe. There are two serious flaws in this argument. Bicycle safety is concerned with *all* possible injuries to the bicyclist, and competent researchers have shown

that the great majority of these injuries, including quite serious ones, were not the result of collisions between moving cars and bikes, but of the bicyclist's failure to control his bike. Of course, that is at least as likely to happen in the backwoods as it is in town, and you'll soon find out that rocks and tree trunks are no more forgiving than curbstones and cars.

The second fallacy is the belief that you'll just be riding in the woods or in the fields, so needn't worry about other road users. You will probably do a very significant part of your riding on roads, just like every other cyclist. You will be riding the roads to get to and from the trail, and you will very likely find yourself using your mountain bike for local transportation, perhaps also for commuting and touring. Even on the trails you will not be alone: there are other

(James Cassimus / BICYCLE SPORT photograph)

cyclists, hikers, rangers and wild animals. You will have to learn to avoid endangering yourself and those others, even if the others appear quite unexpectedly.

If we take a look first at the most serious accidents, those with fatal injury to the cyclist, it becomes obvious that head injury is the thing to fear most. Depending on whose figures you take, anywhere from fifty to eighty percent of all cyclist fatalities are directly attributed to skull and brain damage. As one who has gone through the experience of having his own skull pieced together and refurbished, I can assure you that it is both agonizing and expensive, even if you live through it. Don't be stupid, wear a helmet. And I mean a real helmet, one of the models with a fully enclosed hard outside shell and a thick, firm foam energy-absorbing interior. As a very minimum your helmet should meet the ANSI Z 90.4 standard. Insist on it!

Even a helmet isn't going to save your life with total certainty, so it still pays to heed the recommendations about safe and predictable cycling given in the second part of this chapter. Helmets provide a cushioning effect which prevents the brains from hitting the inside of the skull too severely.

What mushes the grey mass is too sudden a deceleration: anything over 80 G. That is a deceleration of about 2500 ft/sec^2 or, to put it in understandable terms, stopping from 20 mph in less than 0.01 sec. By putting about an inch of absorbing and gradually deforming foam between the skull and the shell of the helmet, you are granted the 0.01 seconds with more likelihood than would otherwise be the case.

Head injury is the biggy, but it's by no means the only (nor, thank God, the most frequent) injury sustained

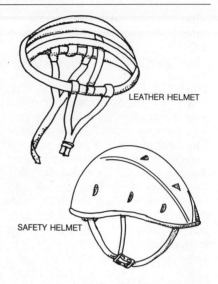

LEATHER HELMET

SAFETY HELMET

by the cyclist. Abrasions, cuts, bruises and bone fractures are all a lot more frequent. All are painful, some require long healing processes, but few are fatal. Almost all are avoidable, though, if you develop the skills outlined in this chapter, and those described in more detail in chapter 6. Let me again emphasize that cyclists get hurt when they fall off their bikes, so that's the thing to avoid. Even those injuries in which a motorist is involved don't usually result from the car crushing the cyclist under his wheels, but from the cyclist hitting either the ground or a part of the car as he falls off the bike.

Some of the most typical minor injuries, which have very much higher frequencies than debilitating head injuries and serious fractures, can be reduced in impact by wearing protective clothing. I'm not suggesting you wear a suit of armor, or even motorcycle garb. But let's take a look at the typical injuries. They are bruises, abrasions and superficial lacerations on the sides of the arms, the shoulders, the legs and the face. If you wear a long-sleeved shirt or jacket and long pants, all made of a strong fabric, and gloves, you will minimize the risk of getting hurt.

Other safety-related clothing advice includes the recommendation not to wear anything that hinders your movements or might get caught in a moving part of the bike. Tuck your shoe laces inside the shoes, your pant legs under your socks, so they don't finish up between the chain and the chainwheel. But also make sure nothing you wear feels uncomfortable when cycling. The latter point is especially important for longer rides, when the jeans you find perfectly comfortable around the house dig into your most valuable parts with every movement of your legs.

If you look at the garb worn by the participants of most cross-country races and tours, you'll notice that my advice is customarily flaunted by quite a lot of those riders. But you'll also see many who take great pains to avoid these hazards. There are no accident analyses available for the relative accident frequencies of the two groups, but I suggest it's smarter to be careful.

Avoiding injuries

However treacherous some people think riding a bicycle is, you won't just fall off it or run into something 'out of the blue'. The causes of falls can be divided into a few distinct categories: diverting, stopping and skidding. A diverting fall occurs when the lean of the bicycle and the direction it is travelling don't agree. Normally, in order to turn right you lean the bike to the same side, which will keep the bike directly under the rider. A diverting fall occurs when you're leaning one way, without also steering that same way: your bike just runs away from you.

This is the kind of thing you learn to avoid when first learning to ride a bike. Kids learning to ride fall off their bikes until they have developed a 'feel' for this method of balancing. Once you know how to ride, diverting falls only happen when the front wheel is unintentionally pushed one way while you're leaning the other. The mountain bike's fat tires make this much less likely to happen than the skinny tires on a regular ten-speed. It still occurs, since you will be riding in more difficult terrain, with rocks and ridges. Avoid this kind of accident, which leads to your very unexpectedly and suddenly hitting the ground, face first, by looking ahead and approaching the obstacles that would divert your front wheel under a steep angle or, better yet, steering clear of them.

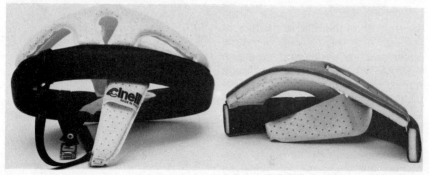

Cinelli bicycle racing helmet: pretty, but offers little protection.

Stopping accidents are just that: the bike stops going forward as it is halted by an obstacle at the front. If you're not prepared for it, your body will keep going, as will often the rear end of the bike. Your rear wheel may lift off, and your body will tend to go forward over the handlebars. This is where a helmet can do you a lot of good, but other injuries, such as those caused by hitting your crotch against the handlebar stem are also frequent in stopping accidents.

Again, looking ahead and anticipating the hazards in your path will avoid most potential accidents of this type. Evaluate the road or trail surface ahead of you, to pick out in advance the kind of obstacles that will be likely to stop your front wheel: deep chuckholes and high ridges, logs and large rocks. It may sound silly, but don't forget that pedestrians, cyclists, motorists and wild animals can be effective bike-stoppers too, with the additional disadvantage of the liability involved in any impact you have on *them*. Try to anticipate where somebody or something might appear suddenly, and keep the liability aspect in mind: given the choice between hitting a car and a tree, opt for the tree. I hope it goes without saying that you should opt for the tree whenever the other alternative is hitting one of God's more fragile creatures, be it man or beast.

Skidding accidents occur when the traction of the tires is insufficient to cope with the forward or lateral acceleration or deceleration. Despite the massive protrusions of tough rubber with which your mountain bike's tires are equipped, this kind of thing will happen quite often under off-road conditions. Your problem will be unpredictable traction on loose and uneven ground. You needn't fall whenever you skid: you can learn to skid in a controlled fashion. But I can't teach you how it's done, because it is a matter of feeling and balance. Like so many other skills, this one too can be mastered only with deliberate practice under increasingly difficult conditions. Get out there and be skidding, and you'll learn to stay on the bike.

The use of the brakes and the steering system play a very important role in skid-control. Going around a bend, you will lose all control if the brakes are locked. Use the brakes to give you the right speed when entering the curve; once in the curve, you'll have enough lateral skidding effect on the rear wheel to worry about, without also having blocked it against forward rotation. True, real gonzo cross-country cyclists can create dramatic clouds of dust and hair-raising cornering effects by doing just that. But you're learning to control the bike for the time being. You too can start practicing the gonzo tricks once you have learned to do the more rational maneuvers.

Cycling Safely in Traffic

Despite most inexperienced cyclists' fears, cycling in traffic is not necessarily tremendously dangerous. In fact, the same kind of things that lead to injuries under off-road conditions cause bicycle accidents in traffic. It is true that most recorded accidents happen on roads. But that is simply the result of the fact that that's where most cycling gets done. Several scientific surveys show that the accident rate per mile travelled is actually *lower* on regular roads, where the cyclist interacts with cars, than it is on paths and trails, with specific bicycle paths being the most dangerous places to be.

The reason roads are relatively safe, despite the presence of fast and powerful motor traffic, lies in their design. Many of the potential obstacles and risks are eliminated from roads, and the behavior of those who use the roads is subject to predictable rules. No trees and rocks, no logs and ditches on the road. Nice smooth asphalt as far as the eye reaches. And because everybody knows he is sharing the road with others, they are forever prepared for the effect others might have on the general situation on the road.

Pedestrians don't suddenly step out into a traffic lane without having made sure nothing's coming their way. Motorists don't turn, cross or overtake, unless they've ascertained they don't get into someone else's way so suddenly as to create a hazard. The position of drivers and riders on the road, and their use of generally understood signals, make their actions predictable. Wherever mutual cooperation alone can not be relied on to solve a potential conflict, the state helps the traffic participants a little: that's how highway markings, traffic signs and traffic lights, rules and regulations came to be.

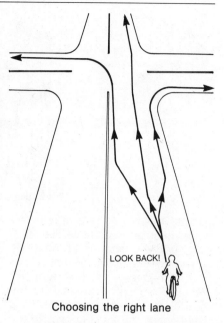

LOOK BACK!

Choosing the right lane

When you are out on your bicycle, adhere to these same simple rules, and use the same sensible instincts you have developed as a motorist. You should first forget some of the 'bicycles-are-different' stories you may have heard as a kid. The cause of accidents is overwhelmingly just the stupid and unpredictable actions carried out by the bicyclists, in the belief that bikes are different. Sure, you have less horsepower and fewer wheels than motorists have. But you don't have fewer responsibilities, and the ones you have are not different from those to which you are subjected as a motorist.

As a bicyclist you will more often be moving slower than other road users. But even that should not lead to different behavior: do the same as you would as a motorist if you were travelling more slowly than others. Leave others room to overtake you whenever it is possible without endangering yourself. Keep to the right when travelling straight; look behind to check on traffic more fre-

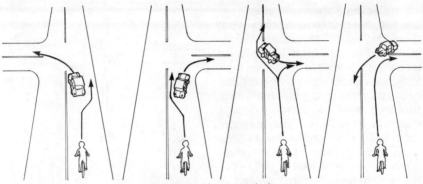

Collision avoidance technique

quently. Most important of all, don't do anything unpredictable, like stopping suddenly, without having made sure nobody is following so closely as to be endangered. Don't turn left without first having made sure the road is clear behind you, giving a clear signal and moving over to the center of the road (or to a left-turn lane) well ahead of your actual turn.

Remember that most of your hazards, certainly if you're going straight ahead, but also once you have properly prepared for any maneuver by having approached the proper position in the road, can be discerned, since they are in front of you. Potential hazards are approaching road users coming the other way, and crossing or turning traffic coming from side roads. Ride far enough out into the road to keep an eye out for crossing traffic. Look well ahead, and scan the edge of the road for clues to the unexpected: car doors opening, pedestrians stepping out, cars ahead of you turning off or pulling up. Look ahead, think ahead, and

use the skills you developed as a motorist, so you will be safe as a cyclist too.

If you are out after dark, you will need lights: at least a clearly visible light in the front and a large reflector in the rear. Don't rely on the assortment of reflectors with which your bike is equipped by the manufacturer: they're not there for your nighttime safety, but merely to satisfy an incompetently conceived federal regulation. More about this in chapter 18, *Accessories.*

The preceding treatment of safe cycling techniques is about as comprehensive as the scope of this book permits. However, there is much more to learn on the subject. The very best source for that kind of information is John Forester's book *Effective Cycling.* Another excellent treatment of traffic sense may be found in John Allen's book *The Complete Book of Bicycle Commuting.* See the section *Further Reading* in the Appendix for further details of these two books.

5
Understanding and Using the Gears

Several years ago an industry survey revealed that some eighty percent of derailleur bike riders never shifted their gears. These people were not conversant with their use and just rode them in whatever gear they happened to be in. Although most mountain bikes to date are bought by more perceptive cyclists, I feel a thorough discussion of the priciple and practice of bicycle gearing will not be lost on many readers.

If you are an experienced rider, or if you have read and understood this same material in one of the many general bicycle books, you may be justified skipping this chapter. All others should not only read these lines, but should also have a bike at hand while doing so, in order to practice what I preach. It's one thing to read about gearing, but it's not going to positively affect your riding technique unless you also develop a hands-on experience.

The purely technical details, such as just how a derailleur works or what are the differences between various models, will not be covered here. A separate chapter is devoted to such matters, namely chapter 15, *Gearing Mechanisms.* Instead, I will explain here what the purpose of gearing is, how it is used, and how to select the right gear for particular circumstances.

The Need for Bicycle Gearing
If you compare the movement of a cyclist with that of a walker, you will discover that the walker has to lift his body weight with every step, while the cyclist just rolls along at the same height. This may be nicely demonstrated by drawing a horizontal line on a wall at the height of the top of the head, and observing the movements of cyclist and walker relative to that line as they move forward, as shown in the illustration.

Cycling is faster at the same output, or easier at the same speed, than walking because the cyclist saves himself the energy required to lift

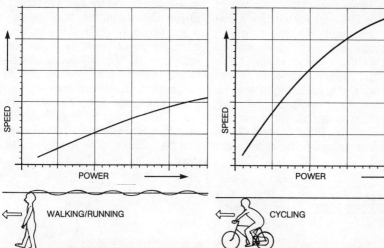

the body weight with every step. Instead, the cyclist has to overcome several other, though lesser, resistances, such as rolling resistance of the wheel and air resistance, which becomes more significant as speed increases. At low power outputs, comparable to walking at a brisk pace, both the cyclist and the walker will be delivering about 60 watt of power (equivalent to about 0.09 hp). On a good level road the walker will progress about 6 km/h (4 mph) and the cyclist will have a speed of 16 to 20 km/h (10 to 12 mph), depending on the type and the quality of the bicycle. These and all other figures given here are based on an average individual; bigger and heavier persons will require slightly more power, lighter and smaller ones slightly less.

Our walker is taking about 130 steps a minute, each with a length of about 75 cm (30 in). If the cyclist's legs move at the same speed as the walker's he will make 65 full pedal revolutions per minute. Through the manufacturer's or the cyclist's own judicious choice of the bicycle's gearing, this situation can be reached at the desired riding speed. It works like this:

Each revolution of the rear wheel will move the rider forward by a distance that equals the wheel's effective circumference. For a well-inflated mountain bike tire that is about 2 m (6 ft 7 in). To reach a speed of 16 km/h (10 mph) at a pedalling rate of 65 revolutions per minute, the rear wheel must cover about 4 m with each crank revolution. So a 26–in wheel must go around twice for every

Thumb shifters (Ross Bicycles Inc. / John Kirkpatrick photograph)

crank revolution, which can be achieved by making the front chainwheel twice as big as the one in the back.

The same could be achieved by making the driving wheel twice as big; it would have to have an effective diameter of 54 in. And that's how the English-speaking world defines bicycle gearing: with the inch-size of the corresponding directly driven wheel, referred to as *gear number*. It's archaic, but so firmly embedded in tradition that I have no hope of changing it. This method dates back to the days bicycles had big directly driven wheels in the front, when it made some sense. For the last one hundred years bicycles have been indirectly driven, which makes the logical measure of gearing the *development,* i.e. the distance travelled per crank revolution. The rest of the world uses this development as a measure of gearing. Development can be calculated by multiplying the gear number by 0.08, which gives a value in meters. Conversely, multiply

LOW GEAR
SHORT DEVELOPMENT

HIGH GEAR – LONG DEVELOPMENT

the metric development value by 12.5 to obtain the gear number in inches. The gear number may be read off from table 1 in the appendix or calculated from the following formula:

$$\frac{\text{chainwheel size}}{\text{sprocket size}} \times \text{wheel size}$$

Let's take a quick look back at the walker. His legs were moving as fast as the cyclist's, but each equivalent 'full revolution' (in the walker's case that would be *two* steps) only covered twice 75 cm or 1.50 m (almost 5 ft). To express this 'development' in terms of a gear number would result in a value of about 19 in – a very low gear indeed. He needs that low gear, because his energy goes less into moving forward than into lifting his body up with every step.

In fact, even the 54-in gear used in the example is somewhat on the low side for cycling on a good level road. Cyclists more typically ride in gears between 65 in and 85 in under such conditions. The riding speeds will be correspondingly higher at the same pedalling rate.

Within his rather low range, the walker has almost unlimited gearing possibilities, by merely varying the

length of his step. Climbing stairs, he goes up almost as much as he goes forward, and takes very short steps of about 30 cm (12 in) each. That corresponds to a 7.5-in gear. He needs that low gear under those conditions, because when climbing he has to lift the weight of his body a much greater distance with every step. Lifting his weight requires additional energy, which is limited by his physical strength and endurance.

The bicycle offers a neat way around the energy loss due to such superfluous weight lifting exercises on a good level road. But bicycles are not self-propelled either, and to climb with a bike also requires the weight of the rider, as well as that of the bike, to be raised. This takes similar amounts of energy to that required when walking up an incline or a staircase. So to go uphill, the cyclist also needs a considerably lower gear.

The bicyclist can't change the size of his wheel, but he can change the speed with which the wheel is driven. It would be very inefficient and tiring to do that by pedalling much slower and pushing harder on the pedals, as must be done on a bicycle without gearing. Instead, the derailleur bicycle offers the rider a choice of

several different front chainwheels and rear sprockets. Combining a smaller chainwheel in the front with a larger sprocket in the back results in a lower gear. A higher gear, which will be desirable when going downhill or with a favorable wind, is selected by combining a large chainwheel in the front with a small sprocket in the back. The concepts 'large' and 'small' are of course relative. The sizes of chainwheels and sprockets are designated by the number of teeth they have, a large one having more teeth than a small one. Sprockets on the rear wheel usually fall in the range of 13 or 14 up to 26 or more teeth for most mountain bikes. Chainwheels usually cover the range from 24, 26 or 28 to 44, 46 or 48.

Although I based most of the preceding discussion on the additional energy required for climbing hills, there are several other factors that may require a lower gear than would be optimal for ideal conditions. In off-road cycling the wheels sink into the ground quite a bit deeper than the inverse effect of deformation or local flattening of the tire where it contacts a hard road surface. This results in a significant resistance, which must likewise be compensated for by selecting a lower gear. Wind resistance when cycling against a strong headwind can have a very significant effect, and should also be handled in a lower gear.

Two often neglected requirements for selecting a lower gear are acceleration from standstill and low-speed riding. When moving off from a stop, the entire mass of bike and rider has to be put into motion, with the wheels not only accelerating forward with the rest of the bike, but also around their own axes. To do that requires a very high power, delivered at a very low riding speed. Both factors require a low gear to minimize the strain on the rider and the bike. When cycling slowly for any reason at all, you will have better control over the bike if you select a low gear, so as not to be pedalling too slowly and to be able to accelerate to a higher speed when appropriate. More detailed instructions on selecting the right gear, as well as the technique of changing gear, will be discussed below.

The Gearing System

To date, only the derailleur gearing system has proven itself in off-road service. Hub gearing, as is used on many northern European bicycles for everyday use, is not considered suitable for various reasons. The components of the mechanism, though

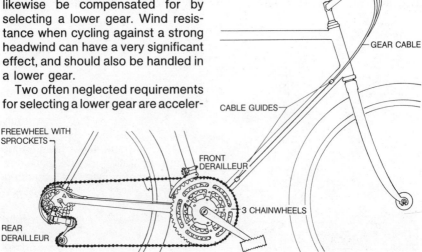

THUMB SHIFTERS

GEAR CABLE

CABLE GUIDES

FREEWHEEL WITH SPROCKETS

FRONT DERAILLEUR

3 CHAINWHEELS

REAR DERAILLEUR

neatly enclosed in the rear wheel hub, are not rugged enough for really heavy service, and the number of available gears, as well as the spread between them, is not appropriate to mountain cycling. Derailleur gearing is therefor the standard on all mountain bikes.

The accompanying illustration shows the components of the derailleur gearing system as used on most mountain bikes. At the bottom bracket three chainwheels are installed; five (or often even six) sprockets are installed on the freewheel, which is connected to the rear wheel hub. The various chainwheels and sprockets each have different numbers of theeth for the chain to engage. The chain can be made to run on (almost) any combination of front chainwheel and rear sprocket, resulting in up to a theoretical maximum of 15 or 18 different gears. The front and rear derailleurs, which are controlled by means of levers on the handlebars via flexible cables, guide the chain sideways to engage the desired combination of chainwheel and sprocket.

The derailleur gearing as it is used on mountain bikes differs in several dateils from that same equipment as it is used on most conventional tenspeeds. Most notably different are the following three points:

1. The gears are controlled from thumb shifters on the (flat) handlebars, whereas on other bicycles the levers are installed on either the down tube, the stem or the handlebar ends.

2. Mountain bikes usually have extremely wide-range gearing, meaning that the difference between the highest and the lowest gears is much greater than it is on most other bicycles.

3. Most mountain bikes have three front chainwheels, whereas most other bicycles have only two; conse-

Sturmey-Archer hub gearing for off-road use, with protective TrailGuard.

quently, mountain bikes are usually said to have 15-speed gearing, rather than the 10-speed gearing used on most conventional derailleur bi-cycles.

Using the Gears

In the present section I will describe the most important points to consider when handling the mountain bike's derailleur gearing. It may be useful to once more check on the points I made in the first section of this chapter, which outlined the reasons for gearing and explained the criteria for selecting particular gears. For purely technical details, such as how the various components of the gearing system actually operate and how they are maintained and adjusted, you are referred to chapter 15, *Gearing Mechanisms*.

To summarize the most important conclusions from the first section of this chapter, you should keep the fol-

The derailleur simply shoves the chain to another sprocket when you change gear.

lowing in mind:

1. Use a *normal* gear of around 65 to 80 inches for normally favorable conditions, i.e. smooth level road and constant speed.

2. Select progressively *lower* gears for correspondingly tougher conditions, such as incline, headwind, rough or soft road surface, and whenever riding slowly or accelerating from standstill.

3. Select progressively *higher* gears for correspondingly more favorable conditions, such as a tail wind or downhill riding.

The maximum and minimum gears available to you are determined by the chainwheels and sprockets installed, as well as by the actual wheel diameter. Assuming a wheel diameter of 26 in, which is standard on essentially all mountain bikes, the typical range of gears for a machine equipped with front chainwheels from 26 to 46 teeth and rear sprockets from 14 to 32 teeth is from a low of 21 in (combination 26 x 32) to a high of 85 in (combination 46 x 14). You will keep in mind that large chainwheels and small sprockets result in higher gears, whereas small chainwheels and large sprockets give lower gears.

Not all combinations can be used to advantage. In particular, the small front chainwheel, often referred to as the 'granny gear', can only be used in combination with the two or three largest sprockets, since the rear derailleur's spring mechanism could not take up the enormous amount of slack that would result in the chain when it lies on the smallest chainwheel and a small sprocket, both front and rear. One other combination which is not desirable is that by which the biggest (outermost) chainwheel is combined with the biggest (innermost) sprocket, since this combination results in excessive twisting of the chain.

To get a feel for the entire system, I suggest you hang the bike up by seat and handlebars or place it upside-down, so you can turn the pedals and the wheels as well as shift the gears while observing what is happening. If you do this by putting the bike upside down, you should raise the handlebars off the ground, so as to clear the thumb shifters for the gears. Stay on the side where the chain is, so you can observe what happens as you activate the gear change mechanisms.

Turn the pedals forward and observe how the chain runs over the chainwheel, around the derailleur and over the sprocket, driving the rear wheel at a certain speed. Now move the shifter for the rear derail-

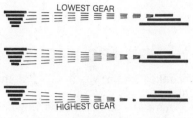

LOWEST GEAR

HIGHEST GEAR

15-speed gearing options

leur (on the right-hand side of the handlebars). Notice how the chain is pushed over to another sprocket and how the wheel turns faster or slower. Shift all the way through from the smallest to the biggest sprocket, a step at a time. Then put the rear derailleur on an intermediate sprocket and shift with the front derailleur by shifting the left-hand thumb shifter.

Shift back and forth until you have developed a feel for which combinations are reached in which shifter positions. If at this point you find there are certain combinations that just don't seem to work (other than the ones I mentioned as unsuitable), or if the chain runs off the chainwheel or sprocket either on the one side or the other, your derailleur will need to be adjusted. You will find a detailed description of this adjustment procedure in chapter 15, or you may take the bike to the store from which you bought it: certainly if this is a new bike, it will be the store's responsibility to get it adjusted right.

Assuming the gears are properly adjusted, you should now take the bike for a ride to practice what you've just learned. Select a medium-low gear, e.g. the middle chainwheel combined with one of the biggest sprockets. Ride on a quiet, level stretch of road, where you feel safe to experiment. Now change into a higher gear by shifting the rear derail-

leur (right-hand lever) to a smaller sprocket, *while pedalling forward without force.* If you do that right, shifting will be as light and easy as it was with the bike stationary. Practice by shifting down, and up, and down, and up again... until you're perfect.

Now shift the front derailleur by moving the left-hand thumb shifter. You will notice that this shift takes longer, because the chainwheel must make fully one half revolution before the chain lies on the other chainwheel. You will also notice how important it is to change while pedalling without applying force to the pedals. That is tricky enough on the level stretch of practice road, and unless you practice a lot and do it very consciously, you will find it almost impossible to do it right when riding in more difficult terrain. The most important point to keep in mind is that you must think ahead: shift down *before* you feel your gear is too high! The other recommendations for trouble-free gearing use are summarized in the following list:

1. Keep all components of the drive-train, especially the chain, clean and well lubricated.

2. Adjust the derailleurs in accordance with the instructions given in chapter 15.

3. Practice gear changing as often as possible: it will get easier and more effective the more you do it.

4. Normally, use only the two bigger chainwheels in combination with the various rear sprockets. Use the small 'granny gear' only for extremely steep terrain, and only in combination with the three or four biggest rear sprockets.

5. Shift step-by-step, rather than across several sprockets at a time.

6. Never try to shift both derailleurs at the same time.

6
Handling Skills and Riding Technique

It is probably safe to assume you know how to ride a bicycle. Just the same, there is a need to discuss some aspects of bike handling and cycling skills, both general and specifically mountain-bike oriented in nature. Of course, it is possible to just get out there and learn by practicing – trial and error, so to speak. But there are smarter and quicker ways to learn any skill than from your own

(David Epperson / BICYCLE SPORT photograph)

mistakes alone, which is what that method boils down to.

There are good reasons why successful performers in any art or sport tend to come from places where many people practice the same. In this respect the Italian and Dutch painters of the sixteenth and seventeenth centuries and the Viennese composers of the nineteenth century are not different from the California and Colorado mountain bike freaks of today. The very best way to learn riding technique and handling skills, in other words, is by joining others who do the same. But I can't deliver the Canyon Gang from Marin County to every household with a mountain bike, so let me suggest you use this book as a substitute. Practice what you read, try to get together with other riders, and you will soon reach the skills needed to enjoy cross-country cycling at its best.

Basic Adjustments
First, get your bike adjusted right; it will increase your comfort and make difficult maneuvers easier. The most rudimentary adjustments were already mentioned in Chapter 3; in the present section I will discuss this matter in more detail. To start off, adjust saddle and handlebars to obtain the relaxed riding position, which is optimal for all riding on level ground. This should form the basis for any further adjustments in response to changes in terrain or riding conditions.

First adjust the saddle height with respect to the pedals. Place the bike close to a wall or a post from which you can support yourself while sitting on the bike. Place the pedal on the far

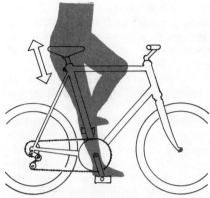

side of the post or the wall, which should be the side where you are standing, in the lowest position (six o'clock). Straddle the bike and try whether you can comfortably reach this pedal while sitting on the saddle with the heel on the pedal and your leg straight. Adjust the saddle height, if needed, by loosening the saddle adjuster quick-release, sliding the saddle up or down and tightening again. Try to pedal backward, still with the heel of the foot on the pedal, making sure you don't rock from side to side. Adjust if necessary.

With the saddle at this height, and still supporting yourself from the wall

Riding posture

or post, place the front portion of the shoe on the pedal and put the pedals in the horizontal position (3 o'clock – 9 o'clock). Now the knee joint of the forward leg should lie either vertically above the center of the pedal or up to 2 in further back. Check this with the aid of an improvised plumb line, e.g. a big bolt or nut hung down from a piece of twine, held from the center of the knee joint. You may use the range of 0 to 2 in to make final adjustment to the saddle's forward position as a function of the saddle-to-handlebar distance, as you find it most comfortable.

Place the handlebars at about the same height as the saddle and try to become comfortable, dividing your weight between saddle and handlebar. If your bike has a separate stem and handlebar (i.e. if the stem and the handlebar are not welded or brazed together, as they are on many mountain bikes), you may find that twisting the handlebars, which can be done after the stem's binder bolt is loosened, may provide a more comfortable position. Tighten the binder bolt again and adjust the brake levers to match the new angle of the handlebars: the brake levers must lie so that you can reach them without twisting your wrists. Make up-and-down adjustments of the handlebars by loosening the stem's expander bolt, tapping on it and twisting the bar into the right position, if it is of the conventional type as used on most bicycles. Some other bars have special clamps with which this adjustment is made.

All the foregoing adjustments should be regarded as temporary: once you get going you may well determine that in the long run slight deviations are necessary for optimal comfort. Just the same, if you don't follow these initial recommendations, you will not have a reliable 'ground base' to which you can refer when fine-tuning the adjustments for the optimal position. It is a good idea to record the adjustments which you find most comfortable in the long run, by engraving the various parts in the appropriate positions. Don't rush it, though: you will need several weeks of regular riding before you can be sure you've found the right adjustments. And these are only the best positions for level riding. Once you get going, you will want to deviate to reflect the differences in terrain.

Handling the Bike

The rather humble art of getting on and off the bike is more important for the mountain bike rider than it is for others. In off-road use, you will find yourself having to dismount suddenly and find it desirable to remount just as suddenly quite often. The way to do that with minimal exertion and risk is by practicing beforehand. Since mountain bikes are made to stand up to more abuse than regular bikes, you may find some of these recommendations contradict what the experienced rider of a conventional

bicycle has learned before. Please keep in mind that I'm telling you here what to do with a mountain bike, not what to do with a twenty-pound racing machine!

The normal way to get on a bike is to stand to the left, holding either the handlebars in the left hand, or the saddle in the right hand. Then you swing the right leg over the seat, the top tube or the handlebars, depending on your own preference and the way you held the bike in the first place. The width of the mountain bike's handlebars precludes the last method, most people finding it easiest to mount by straddling over the top tube. However, the mountain bike's sturdy construction allows you to mount by another and quicker method. To do this, place the left crank in the horizontal position, pointing forward. Hold the handlebars with both hands and place the left foot on the left pedal. Now swing the right leg over the saddle, while your weight, leaning on the left pedal, starts the bike off on its way.

Always start off in a lowish gear: on level roads use the middle chain-

This is the correct way to carry the mountain bike: top tube over the shoulder and handlebar held with one hand (David Epperson/ BICYCLE SPORT photograph)

Shoulder saver on Japanese bike –
a leather strap is more comfortable.

wheel with the largest or second-largest sprocket. Going downhill you may use either the largest chainwheel or an intermediate sprocket. Going uphill you will be best off using the smallest chainwheel with one of the largest sprockets. The easiest way to make sure you start off in the right gear is to think ahead when dismounting: put it in the right gear for getting back on at the time you are ready to get off.

There are also two different methods for getting off the bike, selected depending on whether you intend to continue on foot or not. When you're ready to retire for the day or are stopped in traffic, select a low gear, slow down until you are stopped wherever you want to get off or wait. Move forward off the saddle to straddle the top tube. To get off, either swing the right leg over the seat while holding the handlebars with both hands, or over the top tube while holding the handlebars with the left hand and the seat with the right hand.

If you are getting off in order to walk the bike until you can get back on again, you want to preserve your forward momentum. Get into the right gear for getting back on, slow down until you are going a little faster than trotting pace. Now place your weight on the left pedal, which you keep in the bottom position; swing the right leg over the seat and forward between your left leg and the bike. When you've reached the location and the speed at which you want to dismount, just hop onto the right foot, take the left foot off the pedal and start trotting or walking. The first time you try this you may find your right calf in conflict with the left pedal; overcome this painful problem by leaning the bike more to the left and perfecting your timing.

When you're not riding the mountain bike, you may still be moving forward, either pushing or carrying the bike. Either way, stay on the left-hand side. To push the bike, either hold the handlebars with both hands or just the left hand, while holding the back of the saddle with the right hand. Experience will soon tell under which circumstances to select the first method and when to choose the other. When walking downhill, pushing (not carrying) the bike, keep both hands on the handlebars, in order to fine-tune the braking.

To carry the bike, you may combine the act of dismounting with that of picking up the bike. The moment you hop onto the right foot, reach the right arm down under the top tube all the way until you can place the top tube on your right shoulder, which will slip into the corner of the frame where the seat tube and top tube join. Grab the handlebars with the right hand, so you have the left hand free for balancing and to clear your way.

With a little practice, you'll be able to do all this without stopping, which is not only good if you're racing: it is also more efficient and enjoyable for the casual rider. If carrying the bike on your shoulder hurts, you may either use a shoulder pad, sewn into your shirt or jacket, padding around the frame tubes, or a leather carrying strap installed in the appropriate corner of the frame. Getting back onto the bike later will be as described before, with the difference that the left pedal will be in its lowest position. This is no problem since you have enough momentum to keep moving forward while swinging your leg back over the saddle.

Riding Your Mountain Bike

Riding any bike skillfully is learned, not by reading a book, but by practicing it. Still, it is possible to give some elementary advise which will shorten this learning process to something that can be handled within a short time, provided you practice what you read. There isn't much difference between riding a mountain bike and riding any other bike. In fact, it is somewhat easier, because the fat tires and the relaxed geometry of the mountain bike make this a somewhat more 'forgiving' machine: mistakes which would have thrown you off a racing bike can be corrected gracefully on the fat-tire bicycle.

To ride a bicycle comfortably and predictably, you must understand the bicycle's unique way of steering and balancing. To do that, take the bike for a walk first: push the bike forward, holding it by the saddle only. To make the bike steer to the left, just lean the bike to the left a little; leaning it more will result in a sharper curve. Straighten out the bike by holding it upright, still moving forward. Make it turn to the right by leaning to the right; straighten it out again. Do several rounds on an empty parking lot or any other level area, until you have developed a good feel for the way the bicycle steers and balances. You'll understand that going straight amounts to a series of slight curves, each corrected by the appropriate lean. You'll also realize that this steering technique only works as long as the bike is moving, be it ever so slowly.

Now put this into practice, by cycling very consciously around the same area. Take your hands off the handlebars once you have developed enough speed. You can actually steer your bike that way! Do this several times in progressively more difficult surroundings, until you are quite sure you have control of the bike both at high speed, which is relatively easy, and at very low speeds – even when standing still. After you have developed enough handling skill, start combining these maneuvers with gear changing, as described in chapter 5. Practice until you feel completely in control of the bike.

Next, you will need to develop your stopping skills. You will have used the brakes during the preceding exercises without giving it much thought:

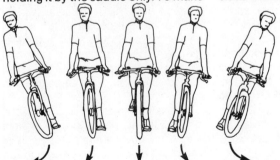

Lean in the direction of the turn. At higher speeds a more pronounced lean is necessary to induce the same curve. At any speed a tighter curve requires more lean.

just pull the levers a little to slow down, a little more to stop, let go when you get going again. But to ride confidently you will need to get a very thorough understanding of the way the bike responds to particular brake applications. First find out which lever controls the front brake (usually, but not always, the left-hand lever) and which controls the rear. Use them one at a time while going straight; notice how the bike reacts in each case. Do the same while riding in a curve. Get a feel for the amount of braking you can do with the rear brake before the rear wheel starts to skid, which is different going straight than when riding in a curve.

Since the combined weight of bike and rider is transferred forward when braking, the front brake is the more effective. Especially when going downhill, you'll need the rear brake too, in order to avoid transferring the weight so far forward that the rear lifts off. To further complicate matters, traction of the tires on the surface varies quite a bit with the nature of the surface. Loose sand and wet surfaces give much less (and less predictable) traction than hard and consistent dry surfaces. Especially when braking hard, keep your body low and far back in the seat. You'll appreciate that only practice will give you a good feel for the right way of braking under any possible condition.

So far, I've only taught you very general skills, the kind of thing you will need whatever type of bike you ride and wherever you ride it. In addition, you should learn at least three specific cross-country skills: diverting, log-hopping and ditch crossing. These are maneuvers which must be performed frequently when riding off-road, and it pays to know how to handle such situations. Inexperienced cyclists who have not learned these tricks find it necessary

to dismount and remount for every one of these obstacles. It is very tiring and actually more dangerous than taking obstacles 'in your stride'.

Diverting is necessary to avoid hitting a suddenly appearing obstacle, when there is neither enough time nor enough room to ride around the obstacle in a wide, smooth curve, as you might do on a normal road. To make a very tight curve, as you will need to do here, the bike must be coaxed to lean quite far in the appropriate direction. Do that by doing what might seem unnatural: first steer the bike very quickly and briefly in the *opposite* direction, and then immediately counter the effect of imbalance thus created by steering sharply the way you want to go. Once you have passed the obstacle, just

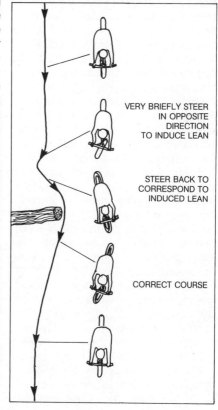

VERY BRIEFLY STEER IN OPPOSITE DIRECTION TO INDUCE LEAN

STEER BACK TO CORRESPOND TO INDUCED LEAN

CORRECT COURSE

lean and steer to get back on course. The illustration shows a diversion to the left of an obstacle; the opposite is done for a diversion to the right. But the drawing doesn't tell you how it feels to do it right: practice until you're perfect.

Log-hopping, also referred to as the 'bunny hop', is a trick which is actually easier on a light, skinny-tired cyclo-cross bike or an even shorter BMX machine, on which it is quite easy to transfer your weight to the back and the front of the bike. However, it can be mastered on a mountain bike too. The secret lies in accelerating while lifting the front wheel over the obstacle by leaning back, and then immediately 'unloading' the rear wheel by throwing your weight up and forward. Practice it by riding straight up to a curbstone; progress to higher and longer obstacles as you improve. This technique is not only used to clear projections, such as rocks and logs, but also to clear narrow ditches and potholes. Practice, practice.

There are two other ways of getting across a ditch or a pothole, selected on the basis of their depth and length. If the depression is narrow or shallow enough not to act as a wheel trap, you kind of ride over the top, doing very much the same as when log-hopping, namely transferring your weight away from whichever wheel is over the ditch next. Choose the shortest way across the ditch to minimize the chance of getting trapped. Whatever you do, don't engage your front brake, even if you are approaching the ditch faster than seems healthy: bending the forks and buckling the wheel are only the mechanical effects of such a mistake – worse may happen to you.

The wider and deeper ditches are taken by riding into them and out again the other side. That can be pretty hairy the first few times, and again it can prove very unhealthy to use the front brake while doing it. Sit far back on the bike and keep your body low. Maximize the length of the crossing by approaching the ditch at an acute angle, picking your way to match your skills and your nerve. Try it out on relatively level terrain at a low speed, before you try your luck on a steep descent. Practice this and a thousand other maneuvers, and some day you'll feel completely at ease, because you know you've mastered the beast.

Standing on the Pedals
Mountain bikes are geared so low that it is usually possible to stay seat-

For really steep climbing, get up from the saddle to keep the front wheel on the ground.

ed on the saddle, even when riding up relatively steep hills. However, even with this kind of gearing it will occasionally be better to get up off the saddle and stand on the pedals. When starting off from a standstill you can accelerate faster and more comfortably if you stand on the pedals during the first few pedal revolutions. This is because at the low speed involved (after all, you're starting off at zero mph), a high force is required at a low leg speed, which is more comfortable if you just lean your weight on the leg that's pushing down.

Another situation which often requires the cyclist to stand on the pedals is during steep climbs. What happens in that case is that the rider's weight rests so far back that the front end of the bike starts to lift off, making the steering ineffective. When the steering becomes noticeably light it is time to get up and lean further forward. On rough terrain this may result in a decrease of the rear wheel's traction. Thus, it becomes a balancing game in which the rider finds the position which allows him to keep pedalling effectively, while still maintaining adequate control over the steering. Practice is what it takes. You will probably find that in the standing-up mode a higher gear can be chosen, since the pedalling rate in this position must be lower.

7
Where to Ride Your Mountain Bike

It is ironic that for a bike which is widely publicized as being built to 'take you anywhere', the question should arise at all; but you may want to know how and where to get the most enjoyment out of your mountain bike. Don't worry, I shall not give you a map of the US with shaded areas to show where you should or should not ride. But I will give you a few guidelines by which you can find suitable areas, and secure access to these places.

Mountain bike or not, the easiest place to ride any bicycle is on well-surfaced level roads. That may contradict everything you've ever heard about the mountain bike before, but it's one of those hard facts of life: if the intent is to go forward, you can't beat roads. Because roads offer relatively direct links between useful places, with good surface quality and minimal differences in elevation, they form the least energy-consuming route to get from A to B, where A may be your house and B some place in the woods.

I'm not telling you to stay out of the woods with your fat-tire bike. I merely suggest you also consider using your bicycle for the purpose *any* bike lends itself to best: transportation. Your mountain bike is only marginally less efficient than a skinny-tired machine on a smoothly surfaced road. It has both advantages and disadvantages in stop-and-go traffic. The flat handlebars and immediately accessible brake levers give you better control. The higher weight of the bike itself, and the wheels in particular, make moving off and changing speed more tiring, but the low gearing compensates for most of that.

The fat tires mean you have to worry less about where you ride: even streetcar tracks, sewer grates and curbstones can be ignored with impunity.

Only for longer distances, especially in areas with strong winds, the mountain bike's forced upright riding position offers disadvantages – at least to the experienced rider. Less experienced cyclists, almost to a man, ride ten-speed bikes in such a poor posture, that they would probably be better off riding a mountain bike, which is at least *designed* for this more upright riding style. There is no law on the books which prohibits the replacement of the flat handlebars with dropped bars; so if you go long-distance touring you may still convert your mountain bike to suit. But as it is, few people really cycle very far, the mountain bike rider probably being no exception. For the distances most people ever want to ride, the mountain bike is quite suitable.

In most areas of the country there is suitable terrain to do real off-road riding within cycling reach. So you needn't necessarily always take your bike in or on the car: ride it there and ride it back. That will give you considerably more cycling experience, and it is a lot simpler. It also makes you a more competent cyclist, which will pay off again when you are cycling off-road. And of course the back woods is not the only goal you should set for your cycling trips: the grocery store, the library or your office are probably just as easily and as enjoyably reached on the bike.

Finding Off-Road Terrain

The mountain bike's characteristics definitely lend it better to off-road cycling than does any other kind of bicycle on the market. In fact, that's how this kind of bike was born: the first mountain bike riders did little else with their machines than ride it down steep, unpaved hillsides at a murderous pace, only to struggle their way back up again to start all over. Sounds silly, but it's a lot of fun. Even if the ride is difficult and the weather miserable, the excitement, the company of other riders, or the beer and bragging afterwards, will keep you coming back for more of the same.

Uphill-downhill cycling is most definitely a group activity. You need the other riders (if only to pick up the pieces and drive you to the hospital when you crash). Standing at the top of a steep hill, waiting your turn while others are taking theirs, is more enjoyable and certainly more educational than doing all that *solo*. Conse-

Touring in the California wine country. (David Epperson / BICYCLE SPORT photograph)

quently, the best places for this sort of riding are probably known to other riders in the area. Ask kids with BMX bikes, if there is no established gang of mountain bike freaks in the area. Challenge someone to the downhill. The BMX kids are excellent candidates for such a challenge; make them try out your bike, and you'll probably have a new recruit to the mountain bike scene very quickly, because your bike will prove infinitely more enjoyable for this kind of use.

If nobody can tell you where to do uphill-downhill riding, find your own locale. You will be surprised to learn that suitable slopes exist in the most unlikely parts of the world. I found half a dozen good places within an hour's cycling from my parents' house in Holland – so don't tell me you live in a flat state, where there aren't any slopes! It mustn't be a thousand-foot drop: riding down the embankment of a high bridge ramp may do the trick. Although you won't find another 'Repack', that Northern California slope which drops 1300 ft in less than two miles, you may discover quite a respectable little slope this way. After all, some of the most challenging and enjoyable slopes in off-road cycling are only one or two hundred feet high, and you're not looking for the ultimate challenge: you're out to have fun.

But there is a lot more to mountain biking than uphill-downhill riding. Especially for those who are more into peace and solitude, cross-country cycling is the more mind-expanding experience. It's my kind of riding, largely also because I'm a cautious old cat, who's taken all the unnecessary risks he wanted to in his day. But not just because I'm a coward: I love the pure thrill of riding where there is no roar of cars to interrupt the tranquility, where all the obstacles are God's, not man's.

Although I like to cycle cross-country alone or with but one companion, this activity is not the exclusive domain of recluses and hermits. In fact, some of the major organized off-road events, with hundreds of participants could be classified as such. There is even a growing number of tour organizers, who scout out routes and take smaller groups of up to perhaps twenty participants through areas you might never have found alone. I can't give any addresses, since it is a fast-changing scene, with people dropping in and out of this kind of thing faster than I care to record. For updated information you may consult the *Fat-Tire Flyer*, other cycling publications, or write to NORBA, the National Off-Road Bicycle Association (all addresses can be found in the Appendix).

True cross-country cycling is quite accessible to most people: you can probably do it quite safely wherever it is not prohibited or where you're not likely to get caught if it is. In the United States enormous areas of land are owned by the Federal Government or individual states and counties, and much of this land is freely accessible to all who do not damage it. And off-road cycling won't do much damage. To quote one converted skeptic from the Southern California Sierra Club, after he was taken on a ride by some local mountain bike enthusiasts, off-road cyclists do "no more damage than Vibram soles, and far less than horseshoes".

That horseshoe-quote is an important one. Equestrians have en icredibly good track record of getting access, even though they ride pretty big and heavy mounts with sharp iron footwear, which can't even be stopped from dropping their wastes whenever they feel the urge. I know of restricted-access watershed areas where horses and their tetanus-carrying excrement are permitted, whereas swimmers, pedestrians and cyclists are excluded. I don't want to get involved in the sociology of public access, but it's not unreasonable to remind oneself that horsey people often have an aura of affluence and influence about them.

Your government at all levels is accountable to all the people, and if you and your mountain biking friends apply enough pressure, have the right arguments and the right attitude, your needs will eventually be met. Whenever access is discussed, be it for horses, hikers or even cross-country skiers, be present to raise your issue. Don't let anybody get away with getting his share, without you getting yours. It will work best if you present yourselves as responsible members of the community, who eat apple pie and watch fireworks, rather than as a bunch of independent near-outlaws.

Make sure to point out that you ride pedal-driven bicycles, not motorcycles. That's often surprisingly enlightening, because American officials and the American public just aren't conditioned to thinking of muscle power when they hear the word 'cycle', certainly if confronted with what is obviously an adult activity. It will also help to be a member of some dignified outdoor or conservation organization, and to make reference to it whenever you present your case.

A particularly touchy issue is that of National Wilderness Areas and the so-called National Wilderness Study Areas. The latter are areas merely considered for possible future designation as Wilderness Area. Although the sign at the trailhead may only prohibit 'motor vehicles', you may soon run into some ranger who'll lay down the law. That's because the 1964 Wilderness Act prohibits the use of 'motor vehicles and other forms of mechanical transport' (while specifically allowing horseback riding). You or I may not think of the mountain bike as providing 'mechanical transport', but Smokey probably does. It's a stupid regulation, and I suggest you contact your Congressman to get it changed, but for now you're stuck with it.

Not everybody has a National or State Forest, let alone a Designated Wilderness Area nearby to worry about. And there are lots of good to excellent places for riding the mountain bike outside such controversial terrain. On the fringes of just about every city and suburb there are areas where paved roads are anything from sparse to non-existent. Such areas may not always be the ultimate cross-country cycling eldorados, but they are almost always quite suitable training ground for the things you will be doing in the woods some day. Besides, you will find such areas more easily accessible. You can

usually identify suitable areas of this kind on a map of the city, especially if you also consult a Geological Survey map of the area, which shows roads that haven't been dignified with a street name, as well as the contour lines to indicate how steep the terrain is.

The ultimate way to find good riding areas goes well beyond the study of a map, though: it's out there, riding your bike, that you'll find the best places to ride. Just the same, I wouldn't go very far without a map. Not just because I'm handicapped with a particularly inadequate sense of orientation. If cycling is to be more than just a kid's game, the real joy is not only to find a place to ride, but also a goal to reach. The map will allow you to venture out more, and to investigate those trails that go further afield, to find other and perhaps better ways back.

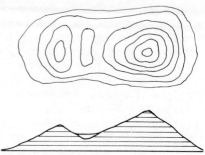

Each contour line corresponds to a "cut" at a certain elevation

On the mountain bike you can take hills, both going up and going down, which other road users wouldn't care to travel. Making the most of this advantage, and not fearing sweat and agony, the true mountain bike rider often discovers quicker, more enjoyable and more spectacular routes away from the regular road. Get out there, and explore!

8
Off-Road Cycling as a Sport

The origin of the mountain bike can be traced back directly to the casually competitive sport of downhill cross-country cycling. Even today, with the number of mountain bikes sold in one year exceeding the million mark, sporting competition still plays a very important role, both in actual use patterns and in further refinement of the equipment. Fat-tire off-road cycling as a sport is definitely here to stay.

One fascinating aspect of this form of cross-country cycling sport is the high percentage of participation. Without even considering the ratio of participants to spectators, which would soon show baseball, football and soccer to be irrelevant sporting events, another participation index is very high in cross-country cycling. Consider the number of ten-speed bicycles in use, and compare it to the number of active participants in any bike race: it's a miniscule fraction of

the total. Yet in many communities around the country a cross-country cycling event will attract so many participants, that one wonders where all those fat-tire bikes came from all of a sudden.

Oddly enough, our kind of off-road competition has developed quite distinctly from an established form of cross-country bicycle racing, called *cyclo-cross,* which enjoys considerable popularity during the fall and winter in most of continental Europe and Great Britain. Yet another form of cross-country cycling, practiced in Great Britain, is called *rough-stuff,* but this has never been practiced competitively as far as I have been able to establish.

In European cyclo-cross racing, aptly termed 'mud-plugging' by the English, light and rather fragile racing bicycles are used. These are equipped especially to make them suitable for the job at hand. Like the

They're off! At the California Rock Hopper race, one of the most popular annual events. (James Cassimus / BICYCLE SPORT photograph)

American mountain bike, they have derailleur gearing and cantilever brakes. These bikes are much lighter and frailer, though, being equipped with racing handlebars and light, skinny tubular tires. The way these bikes stand up to the hard use they get depends less on inherent rugged-ness, as is the case with the modern American mountain bike, than on timely replacement.

In fact, this equipment replace-ment procedure is now driven to the point of absurdity. In many races, competitors not only change bikes after every lap of the short course, to give the mechanics a chance to get them back in order before the next lap, but some riders even use differ-ent bikes for different *sections* of the course. As is so often the case, the American apprentices are actually the ones who outdo their European masters in this respect, and the modern mountain bike is perhaps in a way also a logical reaction to this ludicrous process of scurrying bikes to and from riders along a one- or two-mile course.

Whatever the reason, it was prob-ably the California bicycle racer and mountain bike pioneer Gary Fisher who first served notice to the world of cyclo-cross that mountain bikes were for real. As he had done before, he showed up for the 1980 Northern California Cyclo-Cross Champion-ships with his custom-built mountain bike, and ran away with the senior championship. Though fat-tire bikes had done well in cross-country races as early as 1979, this was the first big success for the concept of fat tires. If you consider that in conventional cyclo-cross the terrain is typically not only rough, but also so muddy and generally unpassable that bikes are carried up to a third of the total dis-tance, such successes for the heav-ier fat-tire bike are quite impressive.

Before you get too jubilant about the superiority of the mountain bike, though, I should also point out that some riders on skinny-tired cyclo-cross machines have done quite well in several mountain bike races. There is also a certain trend away from the 'pure' mountain bike as some people like to think of them. Increasing numbers of competitors are showing up with bikes which are equipped with dropped racing handlebars; some riders use racing pedals with toe-clips, and there seems to be a trend towards less voluminous tires with less dramatic rubber protru-sions. At this point it is still hard to say whether one trend is more suitable than the other, but I suspect it's part-ly a matter of personal preference, partly a function of weather and ter-rain conditions encountered in a par-ticular event.

Whatever the particular equip-ment used to the greatest advantage

European cyclo-cross at its cold and muddy best. This is several-time world champion Roland Liboton of Belgium. (H.A. Roth photograph)

for certain forms of competition may be, I hope our brand of off-road racing will never allow substitution of equipment along the course. Let the policy be that you finish on what you start on, as was indeed one of the first proposed rules when NORBA, the National Off-Road Bicycle Association, was organized early 1983. Up to that time off-road races were either ABA sanctioned (the ABA is the BMX-organization), which meant some form of head protection and gloves were to be worn, USCF sanctioned (i.e. they were regular cyclocross events, also requiring head protection and cycling dress) or privately organized, unsanctioned free-for-alls.

Although the origin of off-road bike racing seems closest to the free-for-all, the number of events and the number of participants to each event had grown to the point where a national sanctioning organization was absolutely essential by 1983. One of the reasons lies in the complex interrelationship of access, liability and insurance. To get access to public lands for any competitive event, the organizers have to accept the liability by providing adequate insurance to cover participants, spectators and others. But to buy insurance for any one event could cost several hundred dollars (so that's where your participation fees went – not into the pockets of unscrupulous organizers, as some riders have suspected).

A national organization is in a much better position to negotiate favorable insurance terms. Such an organization, by guaranteeing that its members and affiliated event organizers adhere to certain responsible policies and procedures, can obtain a policy that covers any number of events, for perhaps less than a thousand dollars. Thus individual organizers can buy what amounts to shares

of this general coverage from the sanctioning organization at very much more favorable rates, and so qualify for obtaining access to public lands more easily.

This was common knowledge in mountain bike circles for a long time, but nobody seemed to be willing to put his money where his mouth was, except off-road race organizer Glenn Odell. Unfortunately, what happened unknown to the membership only six months after the organization was formed, amounted as much to a sellout of the organization as it was a sensible decision to put it on a solid footing. Odell offered to pay off the organization's debts in return for his receiving sole proprietory rights to the association.

That did of course have the very desirable effect that the insurance issue and all related matters could finally be resolved. On the other hand, the entire membership of a rapidly growing organization was disenfranchised in one fell swoop. Perhaps Odell and the other board members who, though with honorable intentions, neglected to keep membership rights in mind, were right in assuming that members are not interested so much in being involved in an organization, but merely wanted somebody to help them organize races. Personally, I don't care to be a member of an organization which doesn't operate democratically. But obviously, if you want to race your mountain bike, and certainly if you want to organize any event yourself, you'll have to face up to it: unless someone else starts a competing organization, NORBA is the backing to have.

Types of Off-Road Events
No, I can't teach you how to race or how to be successful in any of the other off-road events becoming increasingly popular around the

country. You learn by doing, not by reading either my writings or anybody else's. But at least I can give you a little taste of what kind of events are out there to be competing in. Keep in mind that I didn't use the word 'race', but 'event', because off-road cycling is not merely a matter of speed: skill, courage and the joy of simply participating are equally important in this sport.

Competitive off-road events offer the novice the unique opportunity, unknown in almost any other sport, to participate in the same events as the most skillful experts and heroes of the game. Real national celebrities of off-road cycling may be within touching distance – though not for long: they really get going once they get going. In fact, quite a few organizers are beginning to distinguish between the real gonzos and the less experienced riders, due to the problems caused when incompetent riders hinder or even endanger the men and women who are out there for the prizes. However, you can still participate in the same events and it is entirely possible for a talented rider to climb up the ladder of competence to national recognition within a very short time.

Apart from the traditional cyclo-cross events, which involve up to about twenty laps around a virtually impassible circuit, the oldest form of off-road competition is the *downhill* race. Either a steep downhill trail or an open hillside, usually marked to show where you're supposed to ride and where not, is traversed by all riders. Most commonly they all start together; but, depending on the number of participants, they may start in groups or even individually, as is the case in a so-called time trial. The larger the group, the more you rely not only on pure riding skill, but also on conflict avoidance skills (and luck, which may be an essential factor in some mass-start events).

In the *uphill/downhill* race you first have to cycle your way up to the top, before you scramble down as fast as you can. Separate times for the two sections are usually recorded, so there may be different winñers for uphill, downhill, and total distance. Both the pure downhill race and the uphill/downhill event usually take the riders over relatively short routes, largely due to the organizational problems involved in supervising this kind of event when it exceeds a one-way distance of about two miles.

Some mountain bikes are just more comfortable to carry than others. Taken at the Rock Hopper near Santa Rosa, California. (James Cassimus / BICYCLE SPORT photograph)

(David Epperson / BICYCLE SPORT photograph)

Longer events are often billed as *challenges*. Here you may even be offered some flexibility in the choice of the route, with some daredevil invariably finding a shortcut, which will soon be named after him (or her) and as often as not becomes the accepted course of the ride the next time it is organized.

Another event of longer duration is the *enduro*, a lap race of perhaps as many as twenty rounds on a relatively compact course of one or two miles. The course will preferably include different types of terrain. Rather than just overall speed, the placings at the end of each lap are recorded, with certain numbers of points being awarded to the first six riders. Each rider's total points are cumulated for the final placings.

Many off-road bicycle events are *tours*, although they may seem as competitive as any race. Nobody seems to be willing to be the last one home. Several of these tours had become too popular and competitive for the organizers. To take the com-petitive edge off, some organizers now offer their popular tours in conjunction with 'real' races before or after the tour. It is my guess that this will be the most popular form of event in the future, since it gets an interested crowd of potential spectators and a competent body of racers together, which will be rewarding and educating to both groups.

One event which definitely is not a race, but highly competitive just the same, is known as *observed trials*. This form of competition emphasizes skill and has its roots in the motorcycle tradition, as it has been practiced intensively in the New England states. The participants take turns traversing a particularly difficult stretch of terrain, preferably in a wooded hillside area. The whole idea is to complete the course without having to put your foot on the ground. This sport requires rather intensive planning and observation. It's an entirely different type of activity from the speed-and-thrill stuff that was developed in the West.

9
The Mountain Bike
for Touring and Transportation

Any high-quality bicycle lends itself superbly as a means of transportation, and your mountain bike forms no exception to that rule. Although its strengths relative to other bicycles are demonstrated best in rough terrain, its performance still improves as the road gets better. In fact, considering the quality of some of the roads which many cyclists choose to use, one wonders why the conventional ten-speed, used by most casual and regular riders, ever got designed and equipped the way it did, rather than as a mountain bike.

I do not share the view of some mountain bike enthusiasts that other bicycles aren't suitable for anything except racing. I still put in most of my mileage on skinny-tired machines, and enjoy their performance as much as I enjoy my mountain bike's rugged reliability under demanding condi-

tions and on unpaved or poorly surfaced roads. But I do admit to the contention that if I were allowed to choose just one bike for all uses for the remaining years of my life, I'd almost certainly select the mountain bike: it will do anything any other bike can do quite well, and some it can do better.

For that reason I don't propagate the use of different bikes for different purposes, unless cycling is so important to you (as it is to me and most of my cycling friends), that you're willing to spend real time and money on owning, riding and maintaining several machines. If you have a mountain bike, use it for any purpose that seems to lend itself to the two-wheeled mode.

Day-tripping, running errands, touring and commuting are the four stages of progression that lead to competent bicycle use. And that is probably indeed the wisest way to advance, once you are ready to outgrow the exclusive dirt-riding fun on your mountain bike. I'm not suggesting you give up the latter, but, as W.C. Fields once remarked, "I like my cigar too, but I take it out sometimes."

In all of the suggested uses you will enjoy the mountain bike's advantages, especially if you are relatively new to cycling. You will have fewer flats and other mechanical problems than you would on a more fragile machine. You can ride more comfortably on poorly surfaced roads and have less need to pick your way around obstacles and irregularities in the road. You can more easily take shortcuts where there is no road. Due to the bike's relaxed geometry and fat tires, you can maneuver it with more confidence and less risk when you leave the straight and narrow. And finally, the mountain bike is rugged enough to take luggage more comfortably than most other bikes.

Day Tripping

Some call it touring, but experienced cyclists refer to it as day-tripping: the one-day (or part day) ride. It used to be about the only form of cycling known to the American adult. Ride your bike around the countryside, have lunch along the way, and return home before dark.

I purposely left out one part of the description which seemed to be equally essential to most: driving your car to the starting point and back home again after completion of the ride. That's what hikers do, but there is usually no need for cyclists to do the same. Whereas the hiker progresses at the rate of three miles an hour in level terrain and is hopelessly out of place on most main roads, the bike rider gets ahead at about 10 to 20 mph and does very nicely on almost any road he's allowed to use. Even if you live in the middle of a big city, but certainly if you live in suburbia, it will not take all that long to reach pleasant cycling terrain. Besides, it's a real advantage not to have to return to a car that's parked somewhere in the middle of nowhere, or to worry about what's happening to it while you're out riding your bike.

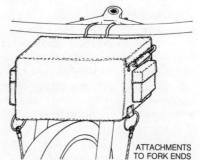

ATTACHMENTS TO FORK ENDS

For this kind of use you can ride the mountain bike the way it is: bare, except for the ridiculous adornment of reflectors, which you probably removed before you took it to the dirt for the first time. That's the way most Americans ride their normal bikes too: no fenders, racks, lights, pump or tools. When it rains or *might* rain they stay home; when they get a flat they get a ride home, and after a few negative experiences they give up on the whole idea. Sure, you can be like everybody else.

But you'll enjoy cycling a lot more if you are better equipped. Take the right clothing (things that are comfortable and don't chafe or pinch) to handle any circumstances you may encounter that day. That includes a rain cape if it might rain: riding in the rain still beats staying home, and carrying a cape even if it doesn't turn out to rain is a thousand times better than staying home when the rain never came. Take some tools, like a tire patch kit, a set of tire irons, an adjustable wrench and a little screwdriver, wrapped up in a rag. Don't forget to carry a pump and at least one full water bottle. Take a lunch if you're not sure you can get food along the way. Carry a detailed map of the area and plan your route ahead of time.

Except for the map, the water bottle and the pump, everything you carry should be put in a bag. Not in a backpack, preferably not in a handlebar bag, but in a firmly mounted bag that attaches to the saddle or to a luggage rack. Handlebar bags, though a lot less hassle on the mountain bike than they are on a bike with dropped handlebars, have very limited carrying capacity and negatively affect handling, steering and braking. Although they are good for small and light items which you want to have handy while riding, I much prefer rear-mounted bags for serious carrying. For day-tripping a good saddlebag with two mounting straps at the back of the saddle, and one to wrap around the seat post, is very useful. But it's not unreasonable to mount a luggage rack in the back and use small pannier bags on either side for such a trip.

How far you travel on a day-tour depends on many factors: your inclination, the terrain, the season, as well as your physical condition and the purpose of the trip, to name the most obvious. Trip purpose is an important factor, because it takes into consideration that you might be interested in other things in life too, rather than just in cycling. Combine your ride with another activity, and you'll have twice the fun. Perhaps the maximum most people can do if pushed lies around a hundred miles in a day, but don't feel bad if you do only thirty, even if you don't combine your ride with a baseball game or a wine tasting party.

Don't be too ambitious on your first few trips: start off with a short half-day ride, progressing to longer all-day rides only when you feel up to it. Carry a water bottle, and don't start out on an empty stomach, because you'll be burning calories. Once you can handle longer trips, make sure you are also prepared for things to go wrong far from home. It will pay to have better maps, more tools, and to mount lighting equipment on the bike in case it gets dark before you have

Mountain bike touring at its best in the mountains of the West. (David Epperson / Bicycle Sport photograph)

made it back home. Only battery lights (or a battery light in the front and a big flat reflector in the back, providing it's not obscured by luggage) lend themselves to mountain bike use – more details in chapter 18.

Running Errands

Libraries and grocery stores, churches and swimming pools are perfectly suitable goals for bicycle trips. Most Americans take their cars wherever they go, even if the distances involved are quite short. Once you start using the bicycle for such errands, you will discover the convenience of this form of transportation for distances of up to say 3 miles. Experienced cyclists go much further, and some day you will too, but for a start three miles is a nice trip: 15 minutes, door to door.

With the mountain bike you can often select (or explore) different routes than those which motorists and other cyclists take. This makes many of these short trips more enjoyable too: you'll be combining off-road cycling with whatever purpose the trip has. In general, though, you will probably be riding urban streets, and to do that it is important to know how to ride safely and wisely. Adhere to my advice about safe riding techniques in chapter 4, *Safety On and Off the Road.*

You will often have to carry something on the bike, be it library books or groceries. When properly equipped, your bike will do that admirably well, but too many cyclists endanger themselves, their cargo and other road users by carrying stuff in their hands. If you don't have a luggage rack and suitable bags on the bike, use a backpack. That's not very suitable for longer trips, but it's a lot better than carrying things in your hands or balancing them on the handlebars or the top tube. If you use a 'soft pack', which sits directly against your back, pack it carefully, with something flat against your back. I keep a flat piece of board, the size of a clip board, in my backpack to keep it comfortable even when loaded with odd-shaped items.

Get to know your way around the city or the area. On the mountain bike you will be a lot more sensitive to unnecessary detours and in a better position to take shortcuts than you were as a motorist. I suggest you always carry a street map on these trips, unless you really know the area like the back of your hand. Although you may have developed a pretty good feel for getting to any point from your house, you'll often want to combine two or more destinations in one trip. Getting from one destination to the other, or even establishing

the best way of combining the two to greatest advantage, will often require consultation of the map. And, of course, that is the best way to get to know your way around even better.

Bicycle Touring

Bicycle touring has been a big thing in America ever since Bikecentennial showed literally thousands of cyclists the way. Today, Bikecentennial is still out there, helping groups and individual members plan their tours. But many more cyclists find their own way here and abroad with varying degrees of success. It's a great way to travel, certainly if you know how it's done right.

Though not originally conceived for long-distance touring, the mountain bike is very suitable for this kind of use. It has better load-carrying and shock absorbing qualities than any other bicycle, it suffers fewer mechanical breakdowns, it has gearing to take on any road and any load. In addition, you can go where others can't. You're not restricted to using the main roads and smooth-surfaced byways, but can combine it with backcountry cycling, not only for the joy of if, but also to get somewhere by a different route or to reach points you couldn't otherwise have reached.

Whatever you've been told elsewhere, one thing is *not* necessary for bike touring: excellent physical condition. It will come as you go along. Just start off with short and easy daily stages. Within days you will feel

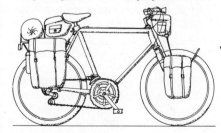

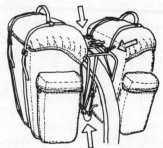

Pannier attachment details

better and fitter, and your skills will have improved to the point where you can tackle progressively more demanding cycling. Certainly if you are carrying a lot of luggage (discussed below and also in chapter 18), you should still keep daily stages short enough to complete in about six hours of actual cycling. This is one of the most important conclusions drawn from the safety survey conducted during the first year of the Bikecentennial tours, where it was found that the likelihood of being involved in a serious fall or accident increases dramatically beyond that point.

What you take along depends on what's ahead. Make sure you are well informed about typical weather patterns in the area of your tour, and don't forget that it gets colder as you go up higher, especially at night. Get information about overnight accommodation: you may want to (or have to) camp out and carry food at least some of the time. Get the equipment to match your needs; but also practice camping out before you leave, if it's only in your own back yard. If you haven't done it before, you'll be astonished how many things have to be considered, but also how many things you can do without.

Make absolutely sure your sleeping bag and clothing don't get wet when it rains. Even if your bicycle panniers and other bags are adver-

tised as being waterproof, they will probably let in all sorts of water at the seams and at the closures. A wet sleeping bag, certainly if it's down-filled, takes forever and a day to dry, and won't keep you warm as long as it is wet. Plastic bags to wrap stuff in, and plastic sheets to cover your belongings during the night, are essential equipment, as is a thin rope to tie things down when it's windy. Consider that at night the soil releases moisture, even if it has not rained in weeks. To be at all comfortable at night you need a waterproof sheet under your sleeping bag, even if you need no further protection.

To carry all your luggage on the bike, you will definitely need racks and bags. There are special racks to fit mountain bikes on the market, but you may be able to adapt a regular rack. In the front your rack should be the type that allows mounting the bags very low, centered around the wheel axles, which results in more predictable steering characteristics. All the bags you use should be mounted so they don't interfere with your movements and so they don't sway. As additional attachments, leather or webbing straps with buckles are more reliable than bungee-cords.

Select the things you take along very carefully, making sure you don't pack incomplete items, things that are too bulky or heavy (use a scale to compare) or superfluous ballast. Plan your route well, and take suitable maps with enough detail for cycling. Practice packing well before you leave and even go for a 'dry run' with the loaded bike the weekend before the tour. You may make the preparatory process more systematic by using a little notebook to record everything you think of, as well as your experiences during the tour. This will make preparing for your next tour that much easier.

Mountain bikers camp out during the annual Crested Butte to Aspen event in Colorado. (David Epperson / BICYCLE SPORT photograph)

Bicycle Commuting

Whole books have been written about the subject of bicycle commuting. Yet I grew up in a household where everybody did it without giving it a further thought. Quite simply it's nothing special once you are a cyclist. You will probably be riding a lot in rather dense traffic, so it's advisable to accustom yourself to that kind of riding. The secret lies in being predictable, as detailed in chapter 4 *Safety On and Off the Road.* And wear a helmet...

Equip your bike for everyday use with luggage carrying equipment: either a rack with panniers or a sturdy big saddlebag. Install lights and a rear reflector if your commute might take you into the hours of dusk or darkness. If you can find fenders to fit the mountain bike's fat tires, it would be good to install them, so you can ride with reasonable comfort even in inclement weather.

It is best to wear really comfortable cycling clothing, which you change for more respectable garb once you get to your place of work, either carrying your civies on the bike or keeping them at work. It's nice to have showers at work, but a wash-down in the wash room will do. As an alternative, you might consider cycling at a more relaxed pace, so you don't arrive perspiring. This may be news to most American cyclists, but all those millions of Chinese and Dutch cycle commuters you've seen pictures of don't have showers at work either: they just pace themselves to feel and smell fresh when they get to work.

Part II
The Technical Side of the Mountain Bike

10
The Engineered Bicycle

This second part of the book is devoted to the technical aspects of the mountain bike and its individual components. I will show you how the bike fits together, how the various parts are ·constructed, how they work, why they were built that way, and finally how to keep them in operating order. This chapter explains in simple terms which technical considerations go into bicycle and component design. In the remaining chapters you'll get acquainted with the individual 'building blocks': frame, steering mechanism, saddle, drivetrain, gearing system, wheels, brakes and accessories.

You may refer to the illustration in chapter 2, which shows the complete mountain bike with the individual components labelled, to refresh your memory. The most obvious differences between it and most other derailleur bicycles are those which make the mountain bike suit-

able for harder use in rougher terrain. These differences are not arbitrarily determined, hoping that if you make everything a little bigger and heavier, the sum total will be more likely to do the job. Instead, both experience and engineering calculations have gone into the design of the bike and its individual components.

Of course, the basic bicycle has evolved the same way. In fact, serious engineering treatises were written as early as the fourth quarter of the nineteenth century. The most successful of these was Archibald Sharp's *Bicycles and Tricycles, an Elementary Treatise on Their Design and Construction,* which is currently available as a facsimile reprint from MIT-Press. Since the end of the last century most mechanical engineering interest has been focused on more ambitious items than the bicycle. But that does not mean research on the bicycle and its con-

The engineered bicycle: Charles Cunningham's Short design, shown off by off-road bike racer Alice B. Toeclips, alias Jacquie Phelan.

struction has ceased. Certainly in recent years, ever since American adults have rediscovered the bicycle, a lot of serious work has been done in this area. The interested reader will find the technical bimonthly newsletter *Bike-Tech,* as well as the book *Bicycling Science,* good sources of current information on technical and physiological aspects of bicycle design (details in the Appendix under the headings *Further Reading* and *Useful Addresses*).

In an elementary engineering sense, it is not difficult to analyze most of the forces that act on a bicycle, to calculate how certain parts should be dimensioned. Although I don't intend to bore the reader with such a detailed analysis, I feel it is in order to at least show what kind of factors enter the consideration. The two crucial elements are the nature and magnitude of the forces applied on the one hand, and the mechanical properties of the materials used on the other hand.

Static Forces

In the simplest case, referred to as static loading (e.g. the bike standing still with the weight of the rider on it), the forces applied on each part of the bike can be easily calculated. Dividing this force through the strength of the material used for each component (and an experientially determined safety factor) will give the cross section that is required to make the part strong enought to stand up to this force. Selecting a stronger material, which can withstand a greater stress without damage, allows the part to be made with a smaller cross section: it will be equally strong but lighter, assuming the two materials have the same density.

Another approach to come up with a lighter design is to select a material with a lower density, e.g. aluminum

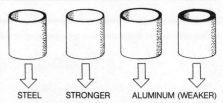

STEEL   STRONGER   ALUMINUM (WEAKER)

The same strength with different materials. Stronger materials require less wall thickness, weaker materials either a greater diameter or thicker walls.

instead of steel. Designing for the same strength, this method will only lead to a lighter construction if the lighter material is not proportionally as much weaker per unit as it is lighter. In fact, it turns out that for many parts certain aluminum alloys can be used to advantage, whereas for other parts, whose nature or form does not permit the use of those same materials, steel alloys may well lead to lighter designs of the same strength. The lighter weight is desirable because it makes the bicycle more efficient in climbing hills, easier to accelerate and to handle.

Metals and Their Alloys

The term *alloy,* which will creep into any discussion of bicycle construction materials, should be clarified at this point. An alloy is essentially a mixture of several different metals. Pure metals are hardly ever used in engineering, since they never seem to have the optimal properties: they are either too weak, too corrosive, or they melt at too high a temperature (the latter being important for brazing materials with which the joints of a bike may be made). One of the ways to improve the properties of certain materials is by mixing in certain non-metalic elements, such as carbon, which gives iron greater strength (and less corrosion resistance, by the way). This does *not* constitute an alloy, but does influence the mechanical properties. Iron with carbon is called steel and is better suited to most uses.

The next step is to mix in small percentages of other metals. Steel is often alloyed with manganese, chromium, molybdenum and vanadium. Aluminum is often alloyed with magnesium, copper and zinc. Brazing rods are alloys containing copper, zinc, silver and cadmium ('silver solder', by the way, is neither all silver, nor even predominantly silver: it just contains more silver than most other brazing materials). Note, if you learn nothing else from this discourse, that 'alloy' does *not* mean aluminum: any mixture of metals is an alloy, whatever the base metal, which for bicycle use is usually either steel (resulting in a *steel alloy*) or aluminum (resulting in an *aluminum alloy*).

In addition to mixing in non-metalic or metalic components with the base metal, the material properties can also be enhanced by means of heat treatment or cold forming. This is most dramatically demonstrated in the case of lightweight bicycle frame tubing. The alloys used for many of the strongest thin-walled frame tubes are in fact not all that exotic. What gives them their phenomenal strength is what's done to them afterwards, usually primarily the result of the forming operation (known as *cold drawing*), or in some cases also by the particular sequence and temperature to which they are heated, and the rate at which they are subsequently cooled (referred to as *heat treating*).

Joining Methods

In the construction of a bicycle frame or other welded or brazed components (e.g. the handlebar and stem on many mountain bikes), the material properties are affected by heating and cooling as a result of the welding or brazing operation. Both these processes require the parts to be heated locally to significant temperatures. In the welding process a very small area is heated to melting temperature, as is a thin metal weldrod of a similar material. The weldrod and the melted metal of the parts to be joined mix and form a solid unit when the weld has cooled off again. In the brazing process the parts are heated over a larger area, though to a lower temperature, namely just above the melting point of the particular brazing rod used. When the brazing material melts, it runs into the narrow gap between the parts and forms the joint when it is cooled off again.

The effect of these heating operations is quite different for different materials and construction methods.

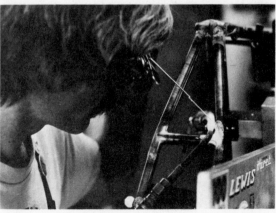

Frame builder Jeff Lindsay at work, brazing the seat stay bridge joint on one of his Mountain Goat bicycles.

Significant is the fact that it is often not so much the joint area itself that suffers, but the so-called *heat affected zone,* just outside the joint. Especially in the brazing process, the temperatures reach a certain point long enough to affect the molecular structure of the metal. Only welding is suitable for aluminum alloys, and a subsequent heat treatment process (controlled heating and cooling in several stages) is required to restore the metal to its design strength.

To compensate for the loss of strength due to the joining operation, but also to e.g. allow welding at all, and to conform to the distribution of stresses within the tube, wall thicknesses must be quite a bit greater at the joints than calculated for the basic structure. On the old American bicycle, like the Schwinn Excelsior, which formed the basis for most mountain bike designs, this greater wall thickness was simply provided by making the entire tube horrendously thick-walled. That results in a rather heavy construction, which will not satisfy the discriminating cyclist. Two things will get you around this problem: use more accurately controlled welding or brazing techniques, and make only the ends of the tubes thick enough, leaving the middle section relatively thin. The latter technique is called *butting,* and this is referred to when the manufactur-

er speaks of *'double butted'* tubing, where 'double' merely means there is a butt at either end of the tube.

Though most of the discussion up to this point has referred to the bicycle frame, similar considerations are equally applicable to the design and construction of other components. Spokes can be double butted to add strength in the most heavily stressed areas just as well as frame tubes. Cranks, handlebars and rims are also shaped or reinforced to concentrate the material where it is most needed, and welding, brazing and other operations apply to many other parts of the bicycle.

Variable Forces

So far, I've only mentioned static forces, the unchanging forces applied to the bike and its components when the rider is merely sitting in the saddle, with the bike standing still or rolling gently along. More significant, and more complicated to determine, are the variable stresses applied by a whole array of different phenomena: the rolling of the wheels and turning of the cranks, the torquing effect of braking, vibration caused by unevenness in the road surface and the veritable jolts and blows caused by the particular abuse encountered when cycling cross-country, not to mention what happens when you run into a fixed object.

Two aspects are particularly significant in this respect: bending stresses and fatigue. Bending stresses occur whenever parts are loaded asymmetrically, whereas fatigue is of particular importance for parts (or specific sections of those parts) which are loaded intermittently. Engineering technology allows the design of bicycles and components so they can also withstand these effects.

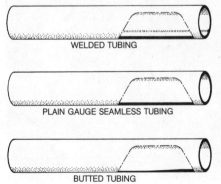

WELDED TUBING

PLAIN GAUGE SEAMLESS TUBING

BUTTED TUBING

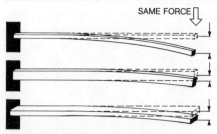

Deflection decreases more with increased height than with increased width.

To design a structure to withstand bending stresses, not only the strength of the material, but also another property, called *modulus of elasticity,* must be considered. This property is virtually identical for any material with the same major alloying component: all steels, from the cheapest to the most exotic, have the same modulus of elasticity. Essentially, this characteristic tells the designer how 'flexible' the material is, i.e. how far it will expand, compress or bend when a certain force is applied per unit of cross section.

In the case of bending forces, it is interesting to note that the dimension in line with the load is disproportionately more effective in restraining the material against bending, although even the width of the item is effective, as the illustration shows: twice as wide a member bends half as much, whereas the same effect can be achieved by mak-

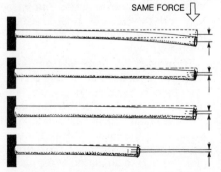

Rigidity increases with greater wall thickness, greater diameter or shorter length.

ing the member only 40 % higher. To translate this into bicycle terms, a tube of slightly greater diameter is more effective in restraining bending than a tube which is equally much thicker. Even so, the wall thickness does resist against bending and flexing. This explains why an expensive light frame, made with strong thin-walled tubing is less resistant to flexing than an identically designed cheaper frame, made of a weaker material, which in consequence requires a greater wall thickness to get the same basic strength.

For the same rigidity, aluminum tubes must be either much thicker or of slightly greater tube diameter.

Aluminum and its various alloys have a much lower modulus of elasticity than any type of steel. Consequently, aluminum parts must be made very much thicker, or still considerably greater in diameter, than equivalent steel parts to resist bending and flexing. Even the alleged 'wonder metal' titanium and its various (expensive) alloys have a lower modulus of elasticity than steel, which again requires the use of thicker walls or greater tube diameters to resist bending stresses, even if the basic strength is quite adequate.

Fatigue is a phenomenon which can cause a part to fail suddenly after it has been subjected to a number of variable loading cycles, close to the material's limiting strength. The most common place for fatigue failure on a bicycle is in the spokes, but handlebars, forks, cranks and wheel axles have been known to fail by this mode. The designer must take this kind of thing into consideration by applying an adequate safety factor and additionally by avoiding so-called *stress concentrations*. These are sudden changes in thickness in a highly stressed part of a component: smooth contours inside and out will reduce the chance of fatigue failure.

Design Geometry

Another factor which enters into the calculations for the strength and rigidity (i.e. resistance against flexing) of a bicycle and its components is the geometry. Your mountain bike is built to more 'generous' dimensions and greater clearances than most ten-speed machines. Since longer parts flex and bend more when the same force is applied to them than shorter parts do, the basic geometry of the mountain bike frame is less rigid. To return the bike to the kind of rigidity which guarantees flexation-free steering and pedalling, greater wall thicknesses and diameters, as well as additional bracing may be required, certainly if one considers the often

Bash plate to protect the drive-train on Range Rider bicycle from Cleland in England.

more dramatic forces applied to the mountain bike. Conversely, less generous clearances may be selected to arrive at a geometry which gives adequate rigidity at a lower weight.

Finishing Processes

Even the finish which is applied to the bicycle's various components has a technical significance. Not only is it intended to keep the bike looking pretty, it also protects the underlying material. In some cases the finishing process actually improves the characteristics of the material. An example of this is the use of intensive anodizing of certain aluminum alloy parts, like the rims. The conventional anodizing process, which chemically oxidizes the surface layer of aluminum alloy parts, only penetrates about 0.005 mm below the surface and merely protects the aluminum from corrosive attack. But anodizing may also be applied to penetrate about ten times deeper, in which case it will significantly increase the hardness and strength of the material. This is indeed done for some rims and also on (expensive) aluminum alloy sprockets on the fanciest and lightest freewheels. Items which are treated this way often look dull-grey and are incorrectly referred to by many distributors as being heat treated. Ninety-nine times out of a hundred they're not heat treated: their greater strength is due to the anodizing process.

To protect the materials, various finishing processes are in use on the mountain bike. Steel parts may be protected by means of painting, chrome plating, nickel plating or zink plating. All the latter processes are usually done galvanically, i.e. by placing the part to be plated and a piece of the plating material in an acid bath and running an electric current

The engineered crank-set from the Cook Brothers. Each crank is machined from one solid piece of superior aircraft type aluminum alloy. (Darryl Skrabak photograph)

through it, which deposits the plating material on the bicycle part. Chrome is the prettiest, but also the most easily destroyed if not kept clean and dry.

Paint finishes can be either enamel, lacquer or epoxy resin. The latter is the most durable, and I suggest it is most suitable for mountain bikes. Some epoxy resin finishes are actually not comparable to paint, but should be seen as coatings, having a much thicker layer. These do not provide quite such a smooth shiny finish, but are by far the most durable.

Aluminum parts are best protected by means of anodizing. This is an electrolytic process in which the surface layer of the corrodible aluminum is converted to a hard and impenetrable corrosion-resistant aluminum oxide. Sometimes a dye is added to the anodizing bath, which renders certain color effects, gold, black and blue being most popular. There is no accounting for taste, but I prefer plain anodizing, which looks just like the aluminum it really is. Especially on an abused mountain bike, plain anodized parts will retain their attractive appearance longer than colored parts, since on the latter every scratch shows up.

I apologize if I have gone more deeply into the technical details of the bicycle and its design than you had gambled on. If the subject doesn't turn you on, feel free to forget the engineering niceties. Just remember that these considerations are necessary to design and build a durable and attractive mountain bike which stands up to the hardships of off-road use, yet is light and maneuverable enough to be pleasant to ride.

11
The Frame

The mountain bike's frame does not look very different from that used on any other bicycle. However, it does differ in some details, as well as in its overall geometry. The illustration shows the mountain bike frame and its components. The main frame consists of four relatively large-diameter tubes: top tube, seat tube, down tube and head tube. The rear triangle consists of a double set of chain stays and seat stays.

In addition to these tubes, there are a number of smaller components used in the construction of the frame. The bottom bracket, which houses the bearings for the crank-set, and reinforcing bridges between the seat and chain stays are oriented perpendicular to the plane formed by the major tubes. Only tubular bridges are sufficiently rigid: flat plates won't do the trick. Drop-outs, which serve to mount the rear wheel and must be at least 6 mm (¼ in) thick to be strong enough, are attached to the points where each pair of chain stay and seat stay join. A clamping device to hold the seat post is installed at the top of the seat tube. Finally there are a number of minor attachments, such

as the bosses for the cantilever brakes, attached to the seat stays, stops, guides and bosses for the brake and derailleur cables, as well as threaded bosses for the installation of water bottles and a rack.

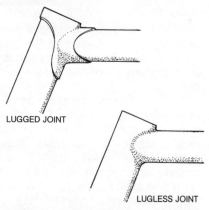

LUGGED JOINT

LUGLESS JOINT

Most conventional bicycle frames are lugged, meaning that the individual tubes are connected by means of brazing them into lugs, as shown in the upper detail above. Many mountain bikes with thicker tubes, which don't fit standard lugs, are made lugless, as shown in the lower detail. The joints may be either brazed or welded. Welding requires the use of

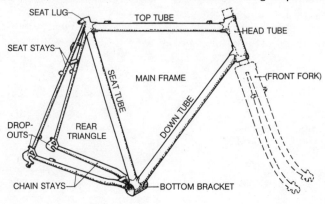

SEAT LUG — TOP TUBE

HEAD TUBE

SEAT STAYS

SEAT TUBE — MAIN FRAME

(FRONT FORK)

DROP-OUTS — REAR TRIANGLE

DOWN TUBE

CHAIN STAYS — BOTTOM BRACKET

tubes with a greater wall thickness, which will generally indicate that it is a heavier and cheaper (though not necessarily inferior) frame. Most of the other attachments are also brazed on, except on some cheap frames, where they may be spot-welded. Continuous smooth contours at the attachment joints are indicative of brazed or TIG-welded joints, while ordinary welded joints often display a rougher finish. Actual gaps are visible in the case of spot-welded attachments.

Frame Geometry

The illustration shows a comparison between a typical mountain bike frame and that of a conventional ten-speed bicycle: the shaded contour is that of the ten-speed. Despite the smaller wheel size (26 in, as opposed to 27 in) and the lower top tube used on a mountain bike for the same size rider, most of the dimensions are actually bigger on the mountain bike. Another difference is found in the shallow angles of the head tube and the seat tube.

The longer wheelbase (typically about 44 in, as opposed to about 40 in

Frame geometry: mountain bike and conventional 10-speed frame

for the ten-speed) serves both to increase clearances and to provide a bike that is easier to handle on steep descents and climbs. Just the same, the last word has not been said about this matter, since mountain bike design is still in its infancy. One of the best handling mountain bikes (certainly for an experienced rider) I have ever ridden is Charlie Cunningham's *Short* design, which does honor to its name, having a wheelbase of 41¾ in. I do believe that the novice rider, who has not yet developed a feel for shifting his weight in response to the bike's behavior, may be better off on one of the long frames.

The total wheelbase is made up of two components: front-center length, measured from the front wheel axle to the center of the bottom bracket, and chain stay length,

Columbus OR frame tubing set; probably the lightest steel alloy tubing set for mountain bikes on the market.

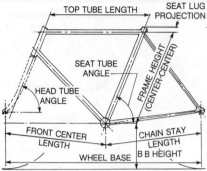

Frame angles and dimensions

74 degrees for a racing bicycle. The seat tube angle and the head tube angle need not be identical. Each designer follows his own reasoning and preferences to come up with a total combination of angles and dimensions which results in different approaches with ultimately very much the same effect: a bike that handles very well in any terrain.

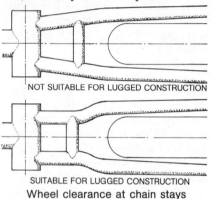

NOT SUITABLE FOR LUGGED CONSTRUCTION

SUITABLE FOR LUGGED CONSTRUCTION
Wheel clearance at chain stays

measured from the center of the bottom bracket to the rear wheel axle. The way the total length is divided over the two depends largely on the seat tube and head tube angles. A frame with shallower angles will need longer chain stays to keep the rider's weight near the center of the bike. This results in a somewhat shorter front-center dimension, assuming both bikes have the same total wheelbase.

Frame angles, or more precisely the angles of the head tube and the seat tube, vary from one model to the next, though they are always less steep than they are on a conventional ten-speed. Typical values are 65 to 70 degrees, as compared to 73 to

Several other details distinguish the mountain bike frame from that of most other modern bicycles. To accommodate a tripple chainwheel and the fatter tires with enough clearance, even when they pick up mud and dirt, most manufacturers

Well built lugged frame on mass-produced mountain bike made by Ross Bicycles Inc. (John Kirkpatrick photograph)

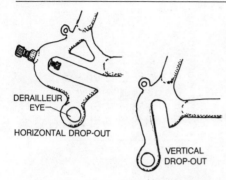

DERAILLEUR
EYE

HORIZONTAL DROP-OUT

VERTICAL
DROP-OUT

install chain stays which are bent into one of the two shapes shown in the illustration. However, it is not impossible (and probably preferable, due to their greater rigidity) to use straight chain stays, which may be locally ovalized or even indented to provide clearance for the wheels and for the chainwheels. The seat stays may be curved slightly to provide the required tire clearance, which should measure at least 5 mm (3/16 in) either side of the tire and at least 20 mm (3/4 in) radially. The radial clearance is also a function of the size and shape of the drop-outs used: make sure the rear wheel can be pushed forward far enough to get it out of the frame, even when the thickest possible tire is mounted.

The main frame differs from that of the conventional bike in that the bottom bracket is usually about an inch higher (12 in off the ground) and the

top tube lower. The higher bottom bracket gives more ground clearance on rough terrain; the lower top tube makes it possible to reach the ground more easily during some of the more hairy maneuvers. One way to solve the latter problem is by installing a slanting top tube which is higher at the front than it is at the back. This solution has several advantages: it allows a longer head tube, which gives a firmer front end and more reliability in steering, and it tends to increase overall frame rigidity – providing the seat post is of a very strong and rigid design, and providing the seat stays join the seat tube at the same point as the top tube.

Frame Materials

To sustain the greater forces to which the mountain bike is often subjected, and which are aggravated by the more generous dimensions of the frame, stronger and especially more rigid (i.e. less flexible) tubing should be used for a good mountain bike frame. As described in the preceding chapter, the latter quality can be improved with the use of greater diameter and/or greater wall thickness, regardless of the quality (and thus the basic strength) of the tubing material. The tubes which are most severely subjected to bending

Straight – i.e. rigid – chain stays on a bicycle built with old style Reynolds 501 MT tubing. The price you pay is sometimes insufficient clearance for fat tires.

forces, apart from the fork, are the down tube and the chain stays. Make sure these are of greater diameter than those used for conventional bicycles, though it can't hurt if the seat stays and the top tube are also beefier.

Table 11-I contains a summary of the dimensions of special mountain bike tubing as manufactured by several tubing manufacturers, compared to the outside diameters used for regular bicycle tubing. For the regular tubing you will note that I don't give wall thickness data, since these vary enormously with the particular strength of material and the purpose of the bicycle. The two dimensions given for the wall thickness of mountain bike tubing refer respectively to the central section of the tubes and the butted ends. These lighter tubing sets use relatively sophisticated materials, though some lend themselves to mass-production techniques, since their high manganese contents render them suitable for automated (i.e. high-temperature) brazing techniques. A frame constructed with this tubing, which can be recognized by the label on one of the tubes, will usually weigh about 3000 gm (6½ lbs), including the fork.

At the time of this writing Reynolds, Columbus, Tange and Ishiwata offer such tubing. Less sophisticated tubing, used on cheaper frames, will give a somewhat heavier frame (8 to 10 lbs including the fork). Such cheaper tubing, often referred to as 'high-tensile', is ordinary carbon steel with a weld seam inside, rather than the seamless steel alloy tubing used for lighter frames.

Some of the cheaper frames are welded together. This is by no means an inferior construction technique. However, welding does require the use of thicker tubing walls. Consequently such bikes tend to be heav-

Table 11-I   Frame tubing dimensions (all dimensions in mm)

Description	Mountain bike tubing (outside diameter and wall thickness)			Conventional tubing (outside diameter)
	Reynolds 501MT	Ishiwata MTB-D	Columbus OR	
Top tube	28.6 (1.0/0.7)	28.6 (1.2/0.9)	28.6 (1.0/0.7)	25.4 (= 1 in)
Down tube	31.7 (0.9)	31.8 (1.2/0.9)	31.7 (1.1/0.8/0.9/1.2*)	28.6 (= 1⅛ in)
Seat tube	28.6 (1.0/0.7)	28.6 (1.2/0.9)	28.6 (1.0/0.7)	28.6 (= 1⅛ in)
Head tube	31.7 (0.9)	33.0 (1.5)	31.7 (1.0)	31.7 (= 1¼ in)
Chain stays	22.2/15.0 (1.2)	28.0/20.0 (1.2)	22.2/14.0 (1.0)	22.2/12.5
Seat stays	14.0/11.0 (0.9)	16.0 (1.0)	16.0/12.0 (1.0)	14.0/10.5
Fork blades	29.8x19.8/15.0 (1.4/0.9)	30.6x20.0/13.0 (1.2)	28.0x19.0/12.5 (1.1)	28.0x19.0/12.5
Steerer tube	25.4 (2.3/1.6)	25.4 (2.7/1.6)	25.4 (2.7/1.65**)	25.4 (= 1 in)

* multiple butting
** helical reinforcing ribs

ier. To save back some of the weight, manufacturers of welded frames often choose smaller outside diameters, resulting in a frame that is more likely to get bent in a spill.

A number of frame builders use aluminum for their frames, Charles Cunningham being the pioneer in this field as far as mountain bikes are concerned. One major manufacturer who uses this material is Cannondale. It would be unfair to talk about aluminum bicycles without mentioning Gary Klein. He is the pioneer in the field and produces probably the finest aluminum frames in the world, although he does not at the time of going to press offer a mountain bike frame.

Successful use of aluminum depends on the smart selection of the particular alloy and the careful balancing of tube diameter and wall thickness, as well as the ability to handle sophisticated welding and heat-treating operations. That makes these items expensive, although the mass-produced Cannondale is re-

markably reasonably priced. Watch the drop-outs on any aluminum frame: they must be big and thick and ugly to do the job adequately; I'd say at least 10 mm (3/8 in) thick.

The complete frame is usually finished with a baked enamel paint, although aluminum frames may be left bare. Enamel is preferable to the slightly transluscent lacquer used on the more expensive conventional ten-speeds, since it is better resistant to the physical abuse associated with mountain bike use. Another suitable finish is epoxy-resin paint, such as DuPont's Imron. Whatever your personal preference, I would still recommend choosing black for any mountain bike frame, since it will be a lot easier to touch up when it gets scratched than other colors.

An excellent way to make a frame for people with short legs – not just for women. (Raleigh Corporation of America)

Maintenance of the Frame

Fortunately the mountain bike frame is a pretty rugged item, which will not easily come to harm. However, it's not indestructible either, so it pays to check its alignment and a few other points from time to time, certainly after it has experienced some extreme abuse. Running into any object big enough to stop it dead, even at a low speed, is likely to cause damage. A serious fall may have the same effect. In many cases it will be the front fork which gets damaged first (see the next chapter), but the frame itself is not immune either.

The weak point on any bicycle frame – certainly if it is treated like a mountain bike – is the area of the down tube, just below the point where it is attached to the head tube. Some of the more conscientious frame builders install either an internal or an external reinforcing pad or sleeve there. Check this point whenever there is reason to suspect frame damage: a bulge, a crease or even merely cracked paint can point to imminent disaster. Go and see a competent frame builder, or let your bike shop do that for you. If the people in the bike shop tell you it can't be repaired, go and find yourself a frame builder who may give you a more qualified answer. Certainly if yours is an expensive machine, it may be worthwhile to replace the damaged tube. That won't be cheap,

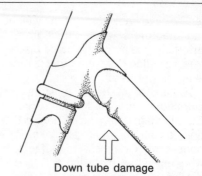

Down tube damage

but still better than buying a new bike.

Sometimes the frame gets distorted through abuse, as evidenced by inaccurate steering or inexplicable scraping of moving parts. When you have established it's neither a bent fork, nor merely a bent wheel or crank, take the wheels out and check for alignment by wrapping a length of twine around the head tube and the rear drop-outs as shown in the illustration. If the distance from the seat tube to the twine measures the same on either side (plus or minus 1.5 mm or $1/16$ in), you can be reasonably sure the frame tubes are not twisted. Then put a steel straightedge along the rear drop-outs, to verify whether they are parallel: the dimension between the outside faces of the drop-outs must measure the same as the sum of the dimensions straightedge-to-tube (measured on the left side), tube diameter, and straightedge-to-tube (on the right).

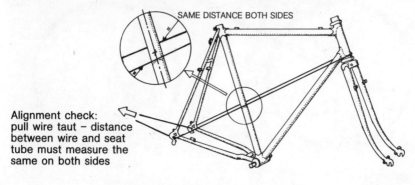

SAME DISTANCE BOTH SIDES

Alignment check:
pull wire taut – distance between wire and seat tube must measure the same on both sides

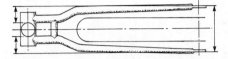

Drop-out check: measure with a long straightedge to verify symmetry.

Don't try to correct frame damage yourself. Even though the procedure often used seems very crude, i.e. bending by hand with the bike held in a vice, it's tricky enough to be left to an expert. This bending technique is politely referred to as *cold setting* and requires quite a bit of experience and a thoughtful approach. If you don't have the requisite faith in your bicycle mechanic (I know one or two whom I'd never trust with a job like that), talk to some friends and find one you have faith in.

What you *can* do yourself is touching up the paintwork. But even that has to be done carefully and con-scientiously. Get matching touch-up paint at the time you buy the bike (certainly if it's not black, which is easy to match). Sand the damaged area with fine sandpaper; wipe clean, apply paint with a small brush only where the paint has been removed (don't overlap), and let dry at least overnight. Don't forget to clean the brush with paint thinner, so it can be used again next time.

The left-hand drop-out on this frame by the German builder Mittendorf is off-set in order to avoid having to dish the rear wheel.

12
The Steering System

The bicycle's steering system consists of front fork, head-set bearings, handlebars and handlebar stem. On mountain bikes the handlebar and the stem often form one single unit. As in the case of the BMX bike, the mountain bike's steering system is subjected to hard use, which is reflected in the heavier construction of all the individual components than usually encountered on conventional bicycles.

Handling Characteristics and Steering Geometry

Your mountain bike, like any other two-wheeled single track vehicle, is not steered by turning the handlebars, as is the case for a two-track vehicle. In fact, given a predictably consistent road surface, the bike can be steered successfully in any desired direction without the handlebar being held. Recall how I recommended getting a feel for the bicycle's handling by 'walking' it, while holding the saddle only. It responds to the inclination of the bike relative to the vertical plane as long as it is moving forward.

The position of the handlebars, following the deviations of the front wheel, changes in response to the lean. At a given speed, a particular lean will point the front wheel under a particular angle. Going faster, a more pronounced lean in the direction of the turn is required to achieve the same curve radius. Going slower, quite a minor amount of lean is enough to turn quite abruptly – all the way down to zero speed, when your bike is 'rudderless', unless you hold the handlebars. The cyclist has to hold the handlebars only for two reasons: to guide it at very low speeds, and to dampen the effect of extraneous influences, such as road surface unevennesses, which would tend to push the front wheel off its course. When you're leaning one way, such an extraneous force could cause the front wheel to point the other way if it were not thus dampened. This would inevitably lead to a diverting type fall.

What keeps your bicycle essentially following its own course is known as *trail*, an element of steering geometry. A bicycle's steering geometry is determined by the head tube angle and the amount of fork rake, as indicated in the illustration. The fork rake is defined as the hori-

Front end of Mountain Goat bike, built by Jeff Lindsay.

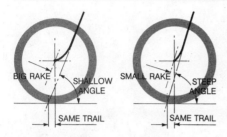

Steering geometry: the same trail with different head angles

zontal off-set between the steering axis and the wheel axle. Usually the manufacturer bends the fork blades to provide the desired fork rake, although other methods may be used. The head tube angle is the angle between the head tube and the horizontal. To arrive at the same amount of trail, a mountain bike with its shallower head tube angle must have a greater fork rake than a racing bike with a steeper head tube angle. Note that increased rake results in reduced trail at any given head tube angle.

To obtain the kind of handling that agrees with off-road use, the mountain bike should have more trail than a conventional bicycle. This will increase the bicycle's tendency to go straight, requiring less force to keep it on course when the front wheel is

diverted by irregularities in the surface. The granddaddy of all mountain bikes, the Schwinn Excelsior, had a 68 degree head tube angle and a 2-in fork rake. This results in a trail of 80 mm (3 3/16 in). Mountain bikes with steeper angles and the same rake will have slightly less trail, making them somewhat more sensitive in their steering characteristics. The graph summarizes the combined effect of head tube angle and rake as reflected in the resulting trail for each combination. All these values are based on the use of 26-in wheels and would be slightly lower for bikes with smaller wheels, higher for bikes with bigger wheels.

The graph consists of two parts. The one on the left gives the conventional trail values, which are measured horizontally on the ground; I refer to these as *projected trail*. An even better predictor of steering characteristics is the variable derived in the right-hand graph, to which I refer as *effective trail*. The latter is the measurable equivalent of what is referred to as *stability index* by some authors. Though the differences between the values for projected and effective trail are only minor, they become greater as head angle values diverge more.

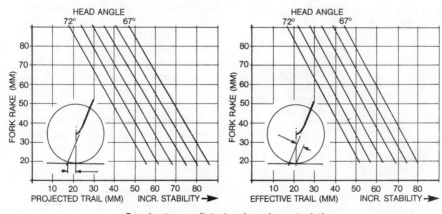

Graphs to predict steering characteristics

The Front Fork

The front fork consists of two fork blades, the fork crown, the steerer tube and the drop-outs at the tips of the fork blades. If any part gets a beating in off-road use it's the fork; consequently the mountain bike's fork should be constructed more ruggedly than the fork for a conventional bicycle. There are a number of methods used for giving the mountain bike's fork the requisite strength.

The fork blades are usually made of heavier tubes. Most fork blade tubing is oval in cross section, and tapered from a bigger oval at the top to a smaller oval or round section at the bottom. Whereas the top of a conventional fork blade measures about 27 mm by 17 mm, special mountain bike fork blades, as offered by most tubing manufacturers, are 2-3 mm bigger in both dimensions, and have a considerably greater wall thickness. Some frame builders use even bigger tubes. My preference is round tubing for maximum lateral stability.

The fork crown must be of a different construction, both so the blades clear the fatter tire and because the bigger mountain bike fork blades don't fit in a conventional fork crown, made for regular fork tubing. Quite a

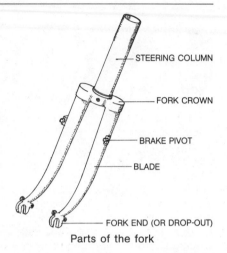

STEERING COLUMN

FORK CROWN

BRAKE PIVOT

BLADE

FORK END (OR DROP-OUT)

Parts of the fork

number of different solutions are in use, ranging from fabricated assemblies to investment castings, and from continuously bent tubing (as used on BMX bikes) to tubular bridge pieces. No solution is inherently superior: strength and reliability depend more on how well the design is executed than on just which design is used.

One solution to reinforce the fork is to run two separate stays from the fork ends to what amounts to a 'second fork crown', installed above the upper head-set bearing. This solution may be familiar from old tandem designs. This method has the slight disadvantage of making adjustment of the head-set bearings more difficult, and the more significant disadvantage that it is rather expensive; I think it's mainly used for its distinguished appearance.

Two other particularly interesting solutions are those used by the Cook Brothers and Charles Cunningham. The Cook Brothers fabricate their fork, which has oval raked blades, by brazing them to a tubular crown piece. Cunningham's very light fork has round unraked blades and a U-shaped tubular bridge piece; the rake is achieved here, not by bending the

Beautiful die-cast steel fork crown for mountain bike use from Cinelli.

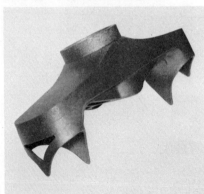

blades, but by attaching them under an angle relative to the steerer tube.

The steerer tube must have the same outside diameter as used on other bicycles to fit the standard head-set bearings. In fact, it must also have the same inside diameter, to match the handlebar stem which is inserted. However, the lower portion of the steerer tube, where it is attached to the fork crown, may (and indeed should) have a greater wall thickness. Reynolds uses a tube that has a butted end with a 2.3 mm wall thickness at the bottom; others make it even thicker, Columbus adding helical ribs. The upper portion of the steerer tube is threaded to install the adjustable parts of the head-set bearings. Although regular forks and head-sets are available

This construction method – often seen on BMX-bikes – is only suitable for forks with very little rake (i.e. bikes with steep frame angles and/or small wheels).

Front fork reinforcement by means of additional braces. It is an excellent, though labor-intensive, way of making a strong front end. This lugless brazed bike is made by the German frame builder Günther Sattler.

with different types of threading (French, Italian and English), all mountain bikes to date use English threading, identified as 1.000 x 24 tpi. This means it has a diameter of 1 in and a pitch of 24 threads per inch, as clarified in the illustration. You may also want to refer to this illustration when I mention other threaded parts in subsequent chapters of the book.

The length of the fork's steerer tube should match the height of the frame's head tube. The correct length can be established by adding the frame's head tube length to the total stacking height of the head-set bearings, as shown in the illustration.

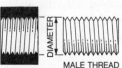

Screw thread details

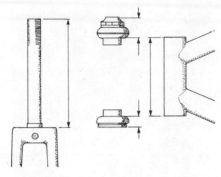

Determining steerer tube length

It may be necessary to shorten the steerer tube of a replacement fork to make it fit. In that case you sometimes also have to get the screw thread cut further, so it accepts the head-set's adjusting parts.

Maintenance of the Fork

There is not much you can do to maintain a fork, except establish whether it is damaged or not. If it looks bent, it probably is, and I wouldn't try to bend it back myself. Take it to a trustworthy bicycle mechanic, i.e. one who doesn't tell you to buy a new bike whenever you have a problem like this.

The steerer tube may be bent if the steering does not turn freely, either all the way or only in certain angles. Check the head-set first (covered in the next section); if things have not improved, take the fork out, which is also described in the next section. Verify with a straightedge whether the steerer tube is straight, and ask your bicycle mechanic for advice if it isn't. When replacing a fork, heed the advice about steerer tube length and threading, given in the preceding section.

The Head-Set

The mountain bike's head-set is similar to the one used for regular bicycles. As shown in the illustration, it consists of a lower bearing and an adjustable upper bearing. A fork race for the lower bearing is installed with a press fit on a little shoulder on the fork crown. The upper and lower bearing-cups are pressed into the head tube ends. The adjustable upper bearing-cup is screwed onto the fork's steerer tube, and is locked by means of a washer, which on many models has teeth to match similar teeth on the adjustable cup, and a locknut which is screwed on top of the steerer tube. The bearing balls, which may be loose or held in a retainer, should be embedded in lubricating grease between the various bearing parts.

Cunningham's unique fork with round blades, which are straight and off-set relative to the steerer tube to get the desired fork rake.

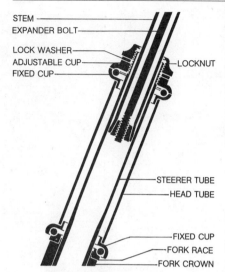

STEM
EXPANDER BOLT
LOCK WASHER
ADJUSTABLE CUP
FIXED CUP
LOCKNUT
STEERER TUBE
HEAD TUBE
FIXED CUP
FORK RACE
FORK CROWN

The parts of the head-set

Head-Set Maintenance and Fork Replacement

These two subjects are covered together, because you can't replace the fork without disassembling the head set. If the object is merely to adjust the head-set, like when the steering feels either too loose or too tight, proceed as follows:

1. Loosen the top locknut about three turns, using a fitting wrench.

2. Lift the lock washer until the teeth (assuming it is a model with teeth) disengage the teeth on the adjusting cup.

3. Tighten or loosen the adjusting cup.

4. Tighten the locknut, while holding the lock washer and the adjustable cup.

5. Check again and readjust if necessary.

If adjusting doesn't do the trick, lubricating, overhauling or replacing the head-set may be in order. When replacing it, get the best you can lay your hands on; the best models I know are OMAS and Specialized. These are better sealed against the penetration of moisture and dirt than other models. Unless the French manufacturers enter the market with different ideas soon, all mountain bikes will continue to use head-sets with English threading (1.000 x 24 tpi, also referred to as 25.4 mm x 24 tpi). To disassemble, remove the handlebars, the wheel and the brake controls; then proceed as follows:

1. Remove the top locknut, using a fitting wrench.

2. Lift off the lock washer.

3. Hold the fork crown and the bottom of the head tube together with one hand, while unscrewing the adjustable cup from the steerer tube.

4. Remove the bearing balls from the upper fixed bearing-cup.

5. Turn the frame around, so the fork is pointing up, still holding the fork crown and the head tube together.

6. Lift the fork out of the head tube.

7. Remove the bearing balls from the lower cup.

If you only want to re-lubricate the headset, clean all the parts, fill both fixed cups with bearing grease (bought from any automotive supply store, or – even better – from a place that deals in boats and outboard motors, since their grease tends to be better resistant against water). Reassemble in the reverse order; then adjust as described above.

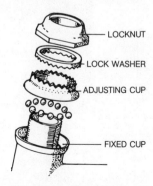

LOCKNUT
LOCK WASHER
ADJUSTING CUP
FIXED CUP

Adjusting parts of head-set

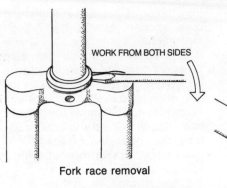

WORK FROM BOTH SIDES

Fork race removal

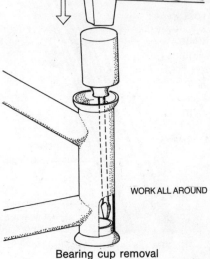

WORK ALL AROUND

Bearing cup removal

To do a more thorough job, necessary if any parts are damaged, you will have to completely overhaul the head-set, replacing whatever parts are damaged, grooved, corroded or pitted. Always replace the bearing balls when you overhaul; measure them up or take one to the store, since different manufacturers sometimes use different ball sizes, although $5/32$ in is pretty much standard. How the fork cone and the fixed cups are removed is shown in the illustrations, as is their replacement.

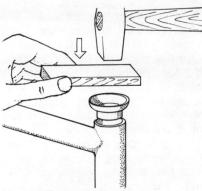

Bearing cup installation

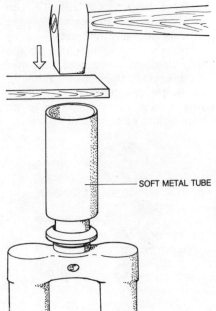

SOFT METAL TUBE

Fork race installation

Handlebar and Stem Maintenance
Next to the tires, the handlebars are what distinguishes a mountain bike most from other, more mundane bicycles. They're flatter and wider. But that's where the similarities between the various mountain bike models end: there are many ways to crack an egg, and apparently as many different ideas of providing strong and comfortable flat, wide handlebars.

The stem is the part which connects the handlebar proper to the fork. It may take many different forms. Some manufacturers braze or weld it together into one fabricated unit with the handlebar. Others take great pains to provide the possibilities of angular adjustment, which are lost if the two parts are welded together. Some follow BMX-practices, by installing a mighty big clamp on the stem, which holds the handlebar with four bolts.

The conventional method of attaching the stem to the fork's steerer tube is by means of one of the two internal clamping devices shown, of which the one with the conical device is probably the more accurately adjustable. The thing is adjusted by loosening the expander bolt in the top, usually with a hexagonal L-shaped bar, called Allen key, which should be supplied or bought with the bike; get the right size: depending on make and model either 6 or 7 mm.

After the bolt has been loosened about four turns, tap it with a plastic mallet (or a steel hammer, protecting the head of the bolt by means of a block of hardwood). Now the stem is freely adjustable. Put it at the desired height and under the correct angle (i.e. straight), hold the stem there, while clamping the front wheel between your legs, and tighten the bolt.

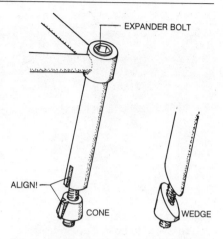

Don't put the handlebar too high: at least 65 mm 2¹/₂in) of the stem should remain below the top of the locknut at the top of the head-set, so it is held firmly.

Some frame builders weld or braze an extension to the inside of the fork's steerer tube, which protrudes from the locknut. They then clamp their special handlebar stem to this extension by means of a sleeve clamp, held in place with several bolts. This kind of solution does not allow much height adjustment: it lends itself only to custom designs which are sized correctly for the discriminating rider.

The handlebar itself is made of tubular material with an outside diameter of 22.2 mm (⁷/₈ in). If aluminum is used, the central section should be reinforced with either an internal or an external sleeve, resulting in an outside diameter of 25 to 26.5 mm there. The supplied width is not sacred: that's what the hacksaw was invented for. A 75 cm (30 in) wide bar not only looks macho, it is also highly impractical: anything over 65 cm (26in) is excessive, The extremely wide bars require the rider to twist his upper body into strange and unstable contortions when riding tight curves at low speed, they easily get stuck

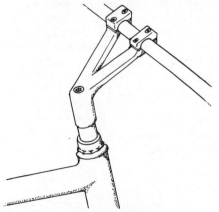

Adjustable handlebar stem

Welded steel combination of stem and handlebar, clamped directly onto an extension of the fork's steerer tube. Also note the brazed-on shift lever bosses.

between two obstacles (if only when you're trying to pass a car in traffic or to get your bike into the house), and are downright uncomfortable to ride in the long run.

If your handlebar is too wide, remove the grips, loosen the brake levers and gear shifters, push those items further in, cut off the ends of the bars to the desired size. Reinstall the grips and tighten the controls in their proper positions, which you'll establish when sitting on the saddle and reaching out for them with your hands on the grips. Use a few drops of dishwashing liquid if the grips don't like the idea of coming off the handlebars.

If you fall off the bike, your handlebar may get bent. It is usually quite alright to bend it back into shape, although you may feel better about letting a bike mechanic do it for you. If you have the nerve for it, first check for cracks or definite folds in the metal – don't attempt straightening a bar which is damaged like that. Use a larger piece of tube, pushed over the end of your handlebar, as a lever. To avoid doing additional damage, it may be wise to only attempt doing

this kind of work on a handlebar which has been removed from the bike. To remove the bar, undo all the controls (brakes and gears) and proceed as for adjusting.

Although I said mountain bikes have flat and wide bars, and that's the way they are sold, that's not the last word about the subject either. Several successful off-road racers equip their bikes with racing (i.e. dropped) handlebars, and do very well, both uphill and down. They usually bend the ends out a little to get a width of perhaps 50 cm (20 in). Certainly for touring over longer distances, I would recommend doing the same. It remains a matter of personal preference, with some flat-bar-riders doing better over a long distance than I do with my preference of dropped bars. Racing bars are usually covered with handlebar tape, which is wrapped around and clamped at the ends with the handlebar-end gear shifters which are used in that case. Grips for flat bars are usually of some plastic foam; I prefer solid rubber or plastic for use in wet weather, where the foam just soaks up the water.

13
Saddle and Seat Post

On the mountain bike you will spend more of your time actually *sitting* on the saddle than you would on a conventional ten-speed. This is the result of the more upright riding style, dictated by the mountain bike's geometry. Whereas on a conventional ten-speed bike the rider's weight is divided over the pedals, the handlebars and the seat, the mountain bike rider's weight often rests nearly fully on the saddle alone.

To be at all comfortable under such conditions, the mountain bike's saddle must be shaped differently than that of the regular ten-speed: wider and softer. So much for theory and logic. In reality, virtually all mountain bikes are equipped with saddles which are fine for ten-speeds, but not for sitting upright. There are better saddles on the market, namely the leather Brooks 66 Champion and similarly shaped leather saddles made by other manufacturers.

Such saddles, shown in the upper part of the illustration, have a substantial leather cover, are narrow in the front and widen near the back to about 8 in. They are supported by means of a strong wire frame with a set of spiral springs in the back. On

the Brooks 66 Champion the longitudinal wire frame is double. Such saddles have just enough springiness to soften the toughest jolts, yet are firm enough not to rock back and forth or sideways under normal riding conditions.

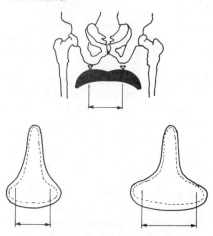

Saddle width requirement

By contrast, the conventional saddle used on most mountain bikes, the Avocet Touring, does not differ substantially from a racing saddle, though it is a little wider and has some foam padding under the thin leather covering. It has a frame consisting of a set of single wires, totally without any springiness. It's not a bad saddle by comparison with what's installed on some of the cheapest mass-production bikes, but it's a far cry from the Brooks 66 Champion. Certainly if you actually ride off-road (remember, that's what your mountain bike was meant to do best), I suggest you convert to the more comfortable saddle, which your dealer can supply, even if he doesn't stock it. How it's done will be shown below.

SPRUNG LEATHER SADDLE

UNSPRUNG NYLON SADDLE

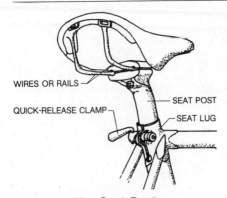

WIRES OR RAILS

QUICK-RELEASE CLAMP

SEAT POST

SEAT LUG

The Seat Post

The saddle is attached to the frame by means of the seat post, which is clamped into the frame's seat tube. Generally, an adjustable aluminum alloy seat post unit is used for even quite cheap mountain bikes. Avoid 'no-name' seat posts: I have known several of those to break off when subjected to the jolts of off-road riding with the rider's weight resting on them. There are quite a number of different solutions to achieve the angular adjustment of the saddle, differing from one make of seat post to

Typical mountain bike seat post with quick-release. The slot in the back should be longer than it is on a conventional bicycle, to prevent the formation of cracks when the quick-release is used frequently.

the next. I'd select a type that can be adjusted from underneath, rather than the ones modelled after the Campagnolo Record type, which are only accessible for adjustment from above, between the saddle cover and the clamp.

This adjustment mechanism not only serves to change the angle of the saddle relative to the horizontal plane, but also allows putting the saddle further to the front or the back. This allows accommodating to the rider's physique, but also to the nature of the terrain, e.g. back to descend, forward to climb. In either case, loosen the mechanism and slide the saddle on its wires to the desired location; check the angle and retighten.

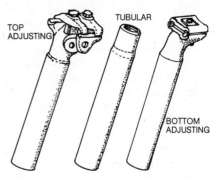

TOP ADJUSTING

TUBULAR

BOTTOM ADJUSTING

Some special mountain bike seat posts are shaped like an inverted L and have a quick-release mechanism for the forward adjustability of the saddle. Many riders find this a useful device. However, it can only be recommended if the seat post is made of forged aluminum. Cheaper models may be castings, which are structurally unreliable: I have known such items to break suddenly.

Items like this could also be made of very light steel tubing. However, that requires labor-intensive fabricating work, which is expensive. It's the kind of thing a custom frame builder can do; also the kind of thing that makes a custom bike so expensive (and qualitatively superior). One solution adopted by several frame builders is to attach a shortened adjustable aluminum alloy seat post inside a long tubular steel seat post. The German frame builder Günther Sattler clamps the two parts together with a handlebar stem expander.

Because the mountain bike should be selected with a low top tube, so there is enough clearance to get both feet on the ground when needed, the mountain bike should also be equipped with a longer seat post than what is used on conventional bicycles. The previously described use of steel tubing is one safe way to make a seat post quite strong and yet as long as it should really be. As it is, most models are only 200 or 220 mm long, which may be inadequate. Choose the greatest length you can get, because at least 65 mm (2 1/2 in) should remain clamped in the seat tube to provide minimally required strength. I suggest you mark the seat post to show the maximum height which leaves 65 mm inside.

The outside diameter of the seat post should match the inside diameter of the seat tube. This dimension is dependent on the frame tubing used. High quality alloy steel tubing, such as the butted tubing provided by Reynolds and some other tubing manufacturers, has a wall thickness of 0.7 mm, which gives an inside diameter of 27.2 mm. To give a positive but easily adjustable fit, the seat post should be no more than 0.2 mm less in diameter. Careful manufacturers ream out the top of the seat tube to provide just the right clearance if the same nominal seat post diameter is used.

Frame builders who use aluminum tubing for their frames have the advantage that the greater tubing diameters, which they are forced to

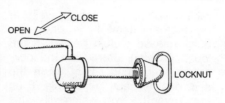

use for adequate rigidity of their frames, also allow the use of a seat post of greater diameter. Thus they can use a light tubular steel post of great rigidity, which may therefore be made extremely long with impunity. That allows them to construct frames which are lower at the seat lug – more like on oversized BMX-frame. This also provides weight savings and great rigidity, as well as an enormous adjusting range for the seat height.

The seat post is clamped in the top of the seat tube. To this purpose the seat tube is slit in the back, and two eyes, attached to either side of the slot, can be clamped together with a quick-release mechanism. On regular bikes (as well as on at least one absolute rock-bottom priced mountain bike I found) a regular bolt with matching nut is used here. Quick-

Seat cluster detail on Mountain Goat frame built by Jeff Lindsay. This type of construction, with the seat stays attaching to the back of the seat tube, is called "fastback".

release bolts are easily available replacement items these days. The quick-release should be set in the 'open' position, after which the lock-nut must be finger-tight when the seat post is freely adjustable. Then move over the lever, which will cause the cam mechanism inside to pull the bolt tight. If the lever can't be turned fully, loosen it, unscrew the locknut perhaps half a turn and try again. Conversely, you tighten the locknut with the lever in the 'open' position if the clamping action is inadequate. To guarantee free adjustability of the seat post, it should be kept lubricated slightly, e.g. with a spray lubricant like WD-40.

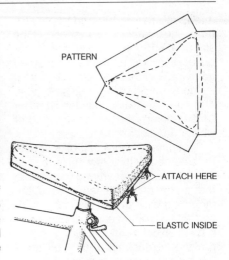

PATTERN

ATTACH HERE

ELASTIC INSIDE

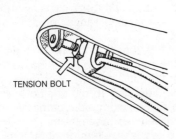

TENSION BOLT

Care and Maintenance of the Saddle

To remove the saddle from the seat post, e.g. to replace either part or to allow cleaning of the void between the saddle and the seat post, it is easiest to leave the seat post clamped in the bike. Undo the adjusting bolt or bolts for the saddle orientation in the top of the seat post; not all the way, though: just enough to remove the seat.

If you want to install a double-wire seat, such as the Brooks 66 Champion, you may have to make a special filler piece to go between the two rails, as shown in the illustration. A

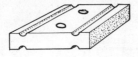

piece of scrap aluminum, a hacksaw, a drill and a file will allow even a relatively unskilled person to make such an item to fit. Surely anybody who works in a bike shop should be able to, if you don't feel up to it yourself.

If you use a leather seat, make sure it doesn't get wet; and if it does get wet, don't put your weight on it until it is dry again. The way to make it relatively immune to occasional moisture is by applying special leather treatment, e.g. Brooks Proofide or – if you're into horses at all – saddle soap. Apply it from the bottom of the saddle cover, i.e. the rough side. When it's really coming down, and certainly if your bike is standing out in the rain, cover the saddle with a waterproof saddle cover, made as shown in the illustration. Use waterproof coated nylon if you want a cover that doesn't tear quickly. If you do nothing more, at least put a plastic bag over the seat when leaving the bike outside if there's any chance of rain. I've seen quite a few leather saddles which were ruined because they were transported on the roof or the back of a car in the rain: carefully wrap plastic around the entire seat to avoid that kind of problem.

14
The Drive-Train

In this chapter I shall present all the parts of the mountain bike's transmission, except for the derailleurs and their controls, which will be treated separately in the next chapter. What will be covered here is the bottom bracket with cranks, chainwheels and pedals, the chain, and the freewheel with its set of sprockets. Although all these items are also used on conventional ten-speed bikes, their application on the mountain bike makes certain different demands on their construction, if they are to be satisfactory under rough riding conditions.

The Crank-Set
For mountain bikes, aluminum cranksets with matching tripple chainwheels and cotterless cranks are used almost universally. Similar parts are used on many fifteen-speed touring bikes, but some additional care should be taken when selecting these for mountain bike use. I shall first show the construction and oper-

Drive-train on mountain bike
(John Kirkpatrick / Ross
Bicycles photograph)

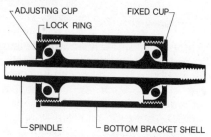

Cross section of bottom bracket

ating principles, and then offer some criteria for their selection.

The bottom bracket spindle is usually supported in the bottom bracket shell by means of two adjustable bearings, as shown in the illustration. The fixed bearing-cup is installed on the chain side (i.e. on the right) and has left-handed screw thread. The left-hand cup may be adjusted to eliminate bearing play, and is then locked by means of the lock ring.

The spindle has square tapered ends, which match similarly shaped holes in the aluminum cranks. The cranks are held on the square ends by means of a bolt or a nut. To allow the chain to clear the fat tires, the chain-side part of the spindle should be somewhat longer than it is on a skinny-tired bike. The crank is threaded internally to accept a tool to extract the crank from the spindle. A dust cap protects the threading. Note that the longer axle-end goes on the side of the chain, to accommodate the three chainwheels. The crank bolts must be tightened from time to time, especially during the first 100 miles or so, when the various parts are still being deformed.

The bottom bracket spindle and its bearings may either be of the ad-

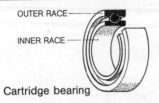

OUTER RACE

INNER RACE

Cartridge bearing

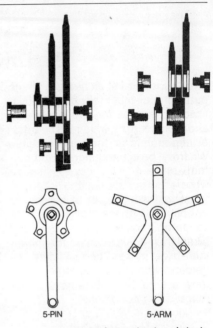

5-PIN   5-ARM

justable type described above, and supplied with most stock crank-sets, or a special sealed bearing unit may be chosen, such as the models offered by SunTour, OMAS and EDCO. These run on more accurate cartridge bearings with superior dust seals. It will be necessary to specify that they are to be used for a tripple crank-set and a 68 mm wide bottom bracket with BCI-threading (also referred to as English threading), which is used universally on all mountain bikes. Another point to watch is the shape of the tapered square end: specify for which make and model cranks it is intended, since the slope of the taper varies between different makes and models, although all will fit after a fashion – but not always accurately enough to provide the correct seating.

Of the many tripple crank-sets available, the French TA company's Cyclotouriste model offers the widest range of replacement chainwheel sizes. However, this model is not as rigid as several of the Japanese models preferred by most mountain bike riders. I find the SR Aerox and GR models, the Shimano DeOre and the Sugino Aero Tour superbly suited to mountain bike applications, though several other manufacturers also make excellent crank-sets.

The two most important points to watch out for are the size of the smallest available inner (small) chainwheel, which should be as small as possible (28, 26 or even 24 teeth), and the integral construction of the right-hand crank with the attachment spider for the chainwheels. Beware of cheaper models, on which a seam is visible between the crank and the spider: these just are not going to stand up to heavy mountain bike use. Selection of the chainwheel sizes, defined by the number of their teeth, will be covered in the next chapter.

The crank length, measured from the center of the bottom bracket spindle to the center of the pedal axle, is the subject of some discussion in mountain bike circles. I am very happy with the standard length of 170 mm, customarily used on most conventional bicycles. However, many riders prefer longer cranks for off-road use, claiming the increased leverage makes it easier to cycle uphill.

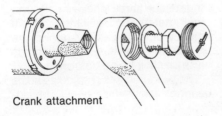

Crank attachment

That is both right and wrong at the same time: longer cranks give more leverage; but crank leverage alone is not the issue: it should be considered in combination with gear selection. In fact, the same overall leverage effect can be achieved with a regular crank and a slightly lower gear. My conclusion from available research data is that people with long legs may benefit from a slightly longer crank (e.g. 175, 180, perhaps even 185 mm), whereas the majority of riders will be best advised to stick with regular cranks.

On the inside of the chain-side crank many manufacturers install a little pin, which serves to pick up the chain if it drops off the biggest chainwheel due to incorrect front derailleur adjustment. It's worth making sure your crank-set has this chain collector, since the chain may otherwise get jammed pretty badly, and will be hard to retrieve. Another protective device is the chainguard-ring, which fits outside the biggest

Mountain bike – English style. This Range Rider from Cleland is very light and elaborately equipped. It is ideal for the wet and muddy English terrain.

chainwheel. American lore has it this thing is intended to protect your pants from the chain's dirt; actually this guard, also known as cyclo-cross ring, serves to protect the teeth of the chainwheel when hit by rocks. Only very substantial items do this satisfactorily. On the English Cleland off-road bikes, the outer chainwheel is even sacrificed and machined down to a bare ring, to serve this purpose. The same manufacturer also installs a substantial guard between the frame and the chainwheels.

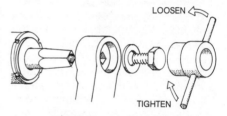

LOOSEN

TIGHTEN

Crank-Set Maintenance

By way of regular maintenance, only occasional tightening of the crank attachment bolts and of the bolts which hold the chainwheels to the spider, as well as checking the bearing play, will be necessary. Check and, if necessary, tighten the cranks. Then check to see whether there is play in the bearings by trying to push the cranks in-and-out. Next, remove the cranks as follows, in order to check for bearing friction or to overhaul the bearings:

1. Remove the dust cap.

2. Unscrew the crank attachment bolt or nut, using a crank tool which matches the make and model of the crank-set, holding the crank firmly.

3. Lift off the washer.

4. Install the puller part of the crank tool, after having made sure the inner portion of that tool is withdrawn fully.

5. Screw the puller into the threaded crank hole by at least 6 full turns.

6. Screw in the inner portion of the puller, holding the crank firmly; this

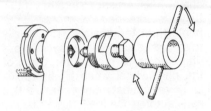

will pull the crank off the axle.

7. Remove the puller from the crank.

To check the bearing adjustment for friction, turn the spindle with your fingers. If you notice any resistance, either all the way or more typically only in certain positions, the bearing assembly must be overhauled. See your friendly bike shop mechanic if yours is one of the sealed models with non-adjustable bearings. Such a unit must either be replaced completely, or must be overhauled by a professional. If you have a standard adjustable bottom bracket, proceed as follows to overhaul and adjust:

1. Remove the lock ring on the left-hand side, using a special tool or a big blunt screwdriver and a hammer, as shown in the illustration.

2. Remove the adjustable cup (or merely tighten or loosen it, if you are only adjusting). Use a special tool or improvise with a metal punch or drift and a hammer, much like you did to undo the lock ring.

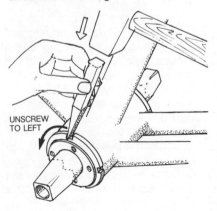

UNSCREW TO LEFT

3. To overhaul, catch the bearing balls; withdraw the spindle, catching also the bearing balls on the other side.

4. Clean, inspect and, if necessary, replace any corroded, pitted or grooved parts.

5. Pack the bearing cups with bearing grease, install the bearing balls (either loose or held in a retainer) in both cups; note which way round the retainer is installed in the illustration.

6. Install the spindle with the longer end pointing towards the chain side.

7. Install the adjustable cup finger-tight.

8. Install the lock ring tightly; then check for play and friction, and re-adjust if necessary, tightening the lock ring while making sure the adjustable cup does not turn with it (easiest to do if you use the special tools for the job).

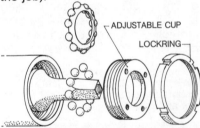

ADJUSTABLE CUP

LOCKRING

Adjusting side of bottom bracket bearing

Some manufacturers use a "one-key release" on some of their crank-sets. This eliminates the need for a separate crank tool, requiring only the use of a 6 mm Allen wrench. Turning the internally recessed bolt to the left will loosen the crank attachment bolt and at the same time push the crank off the spindle. To reinstall, merely place the crank on the spindle and tighten the bolt.

Before installing any crank, make sure all mating surfaces are meticulously clean. Apply a light lubricant sparingly. Place the crank on the square end of the spindle, the chainwheel side on the right, where the spindle should project further. Off-set the cranks 180 degrees. Except for 'one-key' models, install the washer and the bolt. Tighten the bolt with the wrench part of the crank tool. Install the dust cap.

More serious things should probably be left to a bicycle mechanic. He can fix such things as a bent crank and he can straighten out a bent chainwheel. Also the job of overhauling a sealed-bearing bottom bracket usually requires special tools and knowledge.

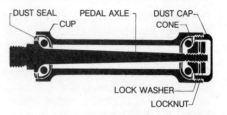

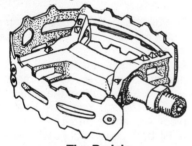

The Pedals

For the bicyclist accustomed to more genteel equipment, the pedals installed on most mountain bikes look rather intimidating. Though I don't recommend plastic models, less viciously ragged chunks of metal will perform quite well, given a fairly big surface, and assuming the rider uses sturdy rubber-soled shoes. Whatever your preference, internally there isn't much difference, as shown in the illustration. Some riders use standard BMX-pedals; others even use racing pedals with toe-clips.

Don't be taken in too easily by references to 'sealed bearings'. Yes, such pedals will have a seal, which increases their ability to keep dirt and moisture out better than a run-of-the-mill pedal. But don't jump to the conclusion that these pedals will all have cartridge bearings with intergral seals: the seal often amounts to no more than a plastic lip or a neoprene O-ring, which closes off most of the gap between the pedal axle and the pedal housing.

To match the enormous threaded pedal hole in Shimano's DeOre crankset, the same company also makes a pedal with a much bigger threaded attachment. This pedal is not originally designed to be used on mountain bikes, being an asymmetric model intended to be used with toe-clips. I wouldn't be surprised if the manufacturer would soon introduce a mountain bike pedal to match. This pedal will follow that manufacturer's DD-design, which is based on the principle that the pedalling action is smoothest if the top of the pedal is

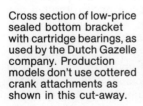

Cross section of low-price sealed bottom bracket with cartridge bearings, as used by the Dutch Gazelle company. Production models don't use cottered crank attachments as shown in this cut-away.

not above the pivoting axis, as it is on all other pedals, but in line with it. Another way to use these cranks with a regular pedal, is to install a bushing which reduces the thread to the standard 9/16 in pedal thread size. By using an excentric bushing, some frame builders provide adjustable effective crank lengths.

As far as maintenance is concerned, you will have to adjust or overhaul the bearings from time to time, namely when they have developed play or are not turning smoothly. For either operation the pedal can be left on the bike. Proceed as follows to adjust:

1. Remove the dust cap.

2. Remove or loosen the locknut.

3. Lift the keyed lock washer and tighten or loosen the underlying cone, after which you tighten the locknut again. Try again and readjust

The biggest name for racing components is Campagnolo. They now also make tripple crank-sets for off-road use, including the Victory, shown here on an Italian Bianchi nountain bike.

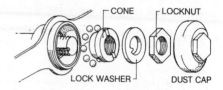

Adjusting side of pedal

if necessary. If this did the trick, you can reinstall the dust cap; if not, overhaul the pedals as follows:

1. After removing dust cap and locknut, lift the lock washer off and unscrew the cone completely, taking care to catch the bearing balls in a rag.

2. Pull the pedal housing off the spindle, catching the bearing balls at the other end.

3. Clean and inspect all parts, replacing whatever is damaged (always use new balls of the right size – usually 5/32 in). You may have to replace the entire pedal.

4. Fill both bearing-cups with bearing grease, making sure they are meticulously clean first.

5. Insert the bearing balls in the cups.

6. Install the pedal housing over the spindle, then reinstall cone, lock washer and locknut.

7. Check and, if necessary, correct the adjustment; finally install the dust cap.

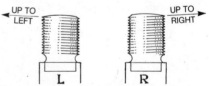

To remove or install a pedal, keep in mind that the one on the left has left-hand threading. Although most pedals are marked correspondingly with an R or an L, the illustration shows how you can tell which is which by looking at the thread: the spiral winds upward to the left on the left pedal, upward to the right on the right pedal. Most pedals are installed using either a thin flat 15 mm wrench on the front, or a 6 or 7 mm Allen wrench from the back of the crank.

The Chain

Mountain bikes use the same kind of chains as other derailleur bicycles. The two different construction methods are shown in the illustration. The major criterion for chain quality is the apparent 'stretch' of the chain after some use. Actually, this is nothing but the cumulative effect of wear at all pins and bushes. It should not be allowed to exceed two percent of the total chain length. If it does, the resistance of the movement between the chain and the sprocket and chainwheel teeth, as well as wear, becomes unacceptable.

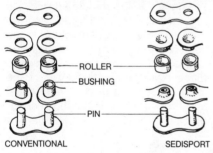

ROLLER
BUSHING
PIN
CONVENTIONAL   SEDISPORT

The chains which are constructed as shown on the right, such as the Sedisport chains, turn out to be incomparably less subject to this apparent stretch. On the other extreme, there are chains such as the Shimano Uniglide, which have 'bulg-

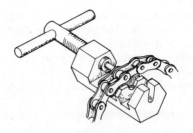

Use of chain rivet tool

ing' link plates. These stretch so quickly and so far, that they are suitable only for light use and low gearing.

All derailleur chains have the same basic link dimensions: $\frac{1}{2}$ in long and $\frac{3}{32}$ in wide, measured between the centers of the pins and between the insides of the inner link plates, respectively. Chains are installed, removed, lengthened and shortened by pushing out one of the pins, using a chain rivet tool as shown in the illustration. Links are added or removed in even numbers. To merely open up the chain for subsequent reinstallation, don't push the pin out all the way, so it is easier to reinstall. If you lose a pin, put in another couple of links and try again.

Chains must be removed frequently on mountain bikes, in order to allow thorough cleaning and lubricating. If you feel play in the links, the chain is worn and should be replaced. Clean by washing out in solvent, brushing between the links. Rinse out in clean solvent; hang out to drip dry over the dish with solvent. Lubricate as soon as the chain is dry, since it may rust if you wait too long. Lubricate with motorcycle chain lube in wet climates, or with synthetic oil or

Chain line

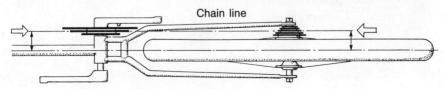

melted paraffin wax in dry and dusty regions (just submerge the chain, leave it there a few minutes, and retrieve using pliers; melt the paraffin wax in a bath of hot water, *not* directly over a hotplate). After installation, loosen the link used for the connection by forcing it in all directions with your hand, so it runs smoothly.

When reinstalling the chain, route it around the rear derailleur as shown in the illustration. To determine the correct length, put it around the biggest chainwheel in the front and the biggest sprocket in the back. In this position the derailleur should have just a tiny bit of 'give' left in its spring tension. If you have really wide-range gearing (or a derailleur which is not up to the job), the chain may hang with a 'belly' in the combination of smallest chainwheel with smallest sprockets. No serious handicap, so long as you don't use these combinations: you really only need the three or four bigger sprockets when the chain is on the smallest chainwheel in the front. If the chain also hangs with a belly in those combinations, you will need a derailleur with a wider range – details in the next chapter.

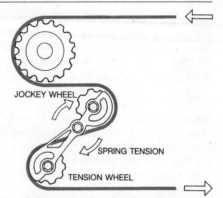

JOCKEY WHEEL

SPRING TENSION

TENSION WHEEL

A final criterion for the correct operation of chain and gearing is the chain line. To allow the chain to engage all the gears with minimal distortion, it should lie in a plane parallel to the bicycle's center when it engages the center chainwheel (assuming tripple chainwheels) and the middle of the sprocket cluster in the back (i.e. the middle sprocket in the case of five, a point between the third and the fourth sprockets in the case of six sprockets). The chain line is measured as the distance between these points and the center of the main frame tubes and the rear wheel hub (between the locknuts) respectively. Let the bike shop take care of any corrections.

Bottom bracket detail with Shimano DeOre crank-set and EDCO sealed bearing spindle.

The Freewheel

Also the mountain bike's freewheel is just like the one installed on any other derailleur bicycle. The illustration shows how it works, but I suggest you don't rush to take it apart: it's full of little bearing balls, pawls and springs. Buy a new one if it doesn't work right and lubrication doesn't solve the problem.

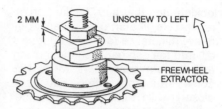

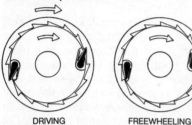

DRIVING   FREEWHEELING

There are quite a few different makes and models, each with its own interchangeable sprockets, which on many models are unfortunately not readily available separately. Shimano and Regina are the ones with the most widely available replacement sprockets. Being able to replace sprockets is useful, since usually only the smallest sprocket wears down fast. Sprocket replacement procedures vary from one model to the next, so I can't give detailed instructions.

If you can't get a replacement sprocket, or to replace the freewheel for other reasons, e.g. because the chain 'jumps' off the teeth of the sprockets, or to obtain a different combination of sprocket sizes, proceed as follows:

1. Take the wheel out of the bike, unscrew the right-hand axle nut, and remove any washers and spacers that may have been used.

2. Place a freewheel extractor (bought in the bike shop, to match the particular make and model of your freewheel) over the splines or recesses of the freewheel around the axle. Reinstall the axle nut, leaving

about 2 mm (³⁄₃₂ in) of clearance between the freewheel extractor and the nut.

3. Unscrew the freewheel by turning the freewheel extractor either of two ways:

a) If you have a vice: hold the tool in the vice, and turn the wheel to the left.

b) If you don't have a vice, clamp the wheel between your body and the walls in a corner of the room, using a big wrench to turn the freewheel extractor to the left.

Do only one turn at a time, then loosen the nut a little, and do another turn, until it comes off by hand.

Before installing any freewheel, clean the screw thread on the end of the hub and inside the freewheel thoroughly. Apply a thin layer of lubricant, match the two threads very carefully and screw the freewheel on with your bare hands. Though freewheels may have any one of three different thread patterns (English, French or Italian), all mountain bikes I've ever seen had English threading (officially known as BCI, and sometimes given either as 35 mm x 24 tpi or as 1.370 x 24 tpi). Make sure you get a freewheel with that kind of screw thread.

To lubricate a freewheel, it must be cleaned externally first. Then hold the wheel on its side, the freewheel

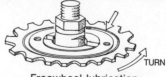

Freewheel lubrication

looking up, the hub resting on a receptacle, like an old tin can. Pour heavy mineral oil (e.g. SAE 90 motor oil) into the gap between the moving and the stationary part, which becomes apparent when you look closely while turning the freewheel with respect to the wheel. Keep pouring in the oil until it comes out clean on the other side; then leave it until it has stopped dripping, after which you wipe the excess oil off the wheel.

UNSCREW TO RIGHT

The only other freewheel maintenance job which I would recommend a novice to try himself is necessary when there is obiously too much play in the freewheel mechanism. Place the wheel on the workbench with the freewheel facing up. Undo the freewheel bearing-cone by turning it to the right (it has left-hand thread), using a pin wrench or a drift and a hammer. When you take the cone off the freewheel, be careful not to lose any of the numerous bearing balls. The bearing play, which caused the wobbling effect of the freewheel, can be corrected by removing one of the thin shim washers which are used to space the cone relative to the rest of the freewheel housing. Screw the cone back on to the *left* (remember: left-hand thread).

15
Gearing Mechanisms

Mountain bikes use derailleur gearing, just like the ten-speed bicycle. Although Sturmey-Archer, the major manufacturer of hub gearing, has made some efforts to convince manufacturers and dealers that hub gears would also do the trick for limited applications, derailleurs remain the obvious choice for almost all off-road applications, particularly where steep hill-climbing is involved.

Derailleur gearing offers great flexibility in gear selection, both in the number of different gears available and in the spacing between gears. The most common arrangement in use today offers more than ten non-duplicating gears between a lowest gear of about 20 in and a highest gear of about 85 in. That makes the highest gear more than four times as high as the lowest gear. For really steep climbing, that lowest gear still offers advantages over walking. You may recall from chapter 5 that level walking offers the equivalent of a 19-in gear, whereas climbing stairs gives an even lower gear.

There are areas in the world where climbing is not the big thing, and there different gearing would make sense. In my attempts to introduce the mountain bike in Holland, where rain, mud and slush, rather than mountains, characterize off-road

cycling, I found dirt on the derailleur system such an inhibitor, that I wished for a five-speed hub gear and a fully enclosed chainguard. Don't worry: in America such rational arguments will never be more powerful than the force of fashion, and if fashion dictates that mountain bikes have fifteen-speed derailleur gearing, then that's what they shall have, even if there's nothing higher than a footstool anywhere on the cyclist's horizon...

The illustration shows the parts of the derailleur gearing system. The front derailleur allows the choice between three different sizes of chainwheels. The rear derailleur allows you to choose between five or six different sprockets. Both derailleurs simply force the chain sideways onto the desired chainwheel or sprocket. The derailleurs are controlled by means of flexible cables from shift

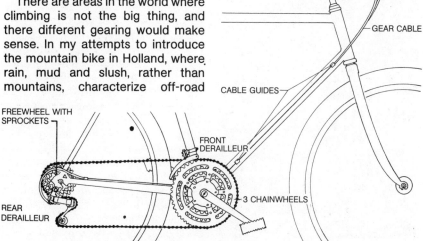

THUMB SHIFTERS

GEAR CABLE

CABLE GUIDES

FREEWHEEL WITH SPROCKETS

FRONT DERAILLEUR

REAR DERAILLEUR

3 CHAINWHEELS

levers on the handlebar; the left-hand lever controls the front derailleur, the right-hand lever controls the rear derailleur. Unlike the levers used on the conventional ten-speed bicycle, the models used on the mountain bike are designed to be shifted with the thumbs, keeping the hands on the handlebar ends, for which reason they are also referred to as thumb shifters.

The Rear Derailleur

Only a limited number of rear derailleur designs is suitable for use with the very wide range gearing used on the mountain bike. The two major Japanese manufacturers, Shimano and SunTour, seem to have a firm hold on the market for such wide-range derailleurs. However, several very fine European derailleurs should not be overlooked: e.g. the Campagnolo Rally and the Huret Duopar, while Simplex also offers several suitable rear derailleurs.

All the various models which are suitable for mountain bike use are

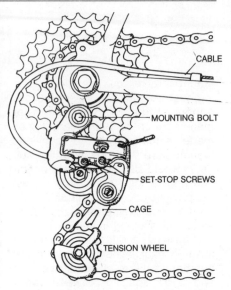

Thumb shifters are standard on mountain bikes. These are from Shimano.

quite similar to the one illustrated. The chain runs over two little wheels, called tension wheel and jockey wheel respectively, which are mounted in a spring-loaded cage, through which the chain is guided. The cage is pivoted at a point somewhere between the two wheels, and can be moved sideways, parallel to the plane of the chain, by means of a set of linkages in the form of a parallelogram. The parallelogram linkage is spring-loaded to extend towards the outside, i.e. towards the smallest sprocket (in catalog language that is referred to as 'high normal'). It is pulled back towards the bigger sprockets by pushing the thumb shifter forward, which puts a stress on the cable.

Adjustment of the range is by means of the two set-stop screws. Turning these screws in limits the lateral travel of the linkage, unscrewing them extends the amount of travel. The second major adjustment is by means of the cable fixing bolt; it allows to increase tension on the cable if slack has developed. Derailleurs made by SunTour have an additional screw, which allows adjustment of the derailleur linkage's angle relative to the chain stays. Correct adjustment of this screw brings the jockey wheel with the chain close enough to the sprockets to ensure smooth shifting.

All mountain bike derailleurs are known as wide-range models. They have very big cages and can reach very big sprockets, while also 'wrapping up' all the chain that comes free when a combination with a small chainwheel and a small sprocket is selected. Two suitable derailleurs which differ in detail are the Huret Duopar, which relies on a double parallelogram system, and the Sun-Tour Superbe Tech, which works on the same principle and has an en-

Campagnolo Rally rear derailleur. The numbers on the cage must be 'translated' to obtain the derailleur's range. It handless all the chain that comes free when shifting from 54x13 to 36x36, i.e. a total difference of 41 teeth. It can handle sprockets from 13 to 36 teeth in the back. (Michiel Sablerolle photograph)

closed linkage system with seal-protected pivots.

Attachment of the rear derailleur is by means of a bolt, which goes throught the derailleur's main pivot point and attaches to an extension of the right-hand drop-out. On cheap (and usually inadequately rigid) drop-outs this derailleur mounting hole is missing; in that case a little adaptor plate is mounted between the drop-out and the derailleur. The most satisfactory results are reached when the drop-outs and the derailleur are from the same manufacturer, since the position of the derailleur and its orientation relative to the wheel axle is then optimized for the specific derailleur used. On cheap bikes the adapter plate should be of the same make as the derailleur for the same reason.

Derailleur maintenance primarily consists of cleaning, adjusting and lubricating. Clean with a mixture of about ten parts solvent to one part mineral oil, after dry brushing or washing off the worst dirt. It works best if you remove the chain first, although some models will allow taking the chain off the derailleur cage without 'breaking' the chain. See the preceding chapter for instructions on chain removal and reinstallation. Route the chain around the derailleur cage as shown in the illustration there.

Lubricating should be done with a very light lubricant, such as WD 40, which is sprayed onto the pivot points, the bearings for the jockey and tension wheels, the cable clamp bolt and the adjustment screws. Don't lubricate without cleaning first, though. At the same time make sure the chain is also properly cleaned and lubricated – see chapter 14 for details.

Derailleur adjustment is necessary whenever you have difficulties changing into particular gears, or when the chain is shifted beyond the biggest or smallest sprocket. Proceed as follows:

1. Set the control handle in the position for the highest gear, making sure the chain actually engages the smallest sprocket.

2. Check and, if necessary, correct the cable tension in this position: there should be neither slack nor noticeable tension on the cable; correct by adjusting either the clamping position of the cable end at the derailleur, or by means of the adjusting barrel provided on many derailleur models: undo the locknut, screw the adjusting barrel in or out, then tighten the locknut again, holding the adjusting barrel in place.

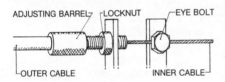

ADJUSTING BARREL⌐ ⌐LOCKNUT   ⌐EYE BOLT

⌐OUTER CABLE   INNER CABLE⌐

Sachs-Huret derailleur with adaptor plate for installation on frames without derailleur eye on the drop-out.

3. Further adjustment is by means of the set-stop screws, which limit the derailleur cage's lateral movement. By observing what happens at the derailleur when shifting, you can determine which of these screws limits travel to the outside, which to

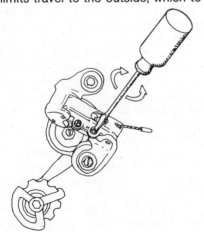

Set-stop screw adjustment

the inside, if you can't find markings H for *high* and L for *low*. If the derailleur was pushed too far in any given direction (leading to 'dumping' the chain), screw the set-stop screw *in* a little, *out* if the chain was not pushed over far enough to reach the appropriate gear.

On SunTour derailleurs you'll find an additional adjustment screw, which is used to modify the angle between the derailleur linkage arms and the chain stays. This adjustment is made with the chain installed and the derailleur set for the highest gear (smallest sprocket). In this position, adjust the screw until the linkage is parallel to the chain stay. This brings the jockey wheel in the most favorable position to guide the chain from one sprocket to the next. Try out all the gears and make any further adjustments that may be necessary.

The Front Derailleur

The principle of the front derailleur is shown in the illustration. A simple chain guide is moved sideways by means of a linkage system, controlled from the left-hand thumb shifter via a flexible cable. Front derailleurs may be of either the 'high normal' or 'low normal' design, depending on the way the spring pushes the cage when the cable tension is relaxed. Most are 'low normal': push the shifter forward to reach a bigger chainwheel, i.e. a higher gear; pull it back towards you to reach a smaller chainwheel, i.e. a lower gear.

To reach down far enough to pick up the chain from the small inner chainwheel used on mountain bikes, the front derailleur must be designed for a wide range, referring to the difference between the biggest and smallest chainwheel (preferably 24 teeth). The old standard for this kind of application is the Simplex model SLJA-523, which has a long and sturdy cage. In recent years Shimano and SunTour, followed more recently by Huret and Simplex, have all introduced models which are even more suitable for mountain bike use, since they are less sensitive to minor movements of the controls. These all have a wider cage and a curved inner plate, which moves the chain over more gently and obviates the need

for frequent fine-tuning with the front derailleur control after each shift with the rear derailleur.

The front derailleur should be installed at the right height to just clear the largest chainwheel, as shown in the illustration. The outside of the cage must be absolutely parallel to the chainwheel. Additional adjustments are by means of the cable tension adjuster and the set-stop screws. These adjustments are similar to those which were described for the rear derailleur. Cleaning and lubricating will also be well rewarded.

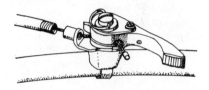

Derailleur Controls

The thumb shifters used to control mountain bike derailleurs are made by both Shimano and SunTour in pretty much the same quality. Similar models are now also available from Huret and Simplex. They have a spring-loaded serrated device inside, which works as a ratchet mechanism. This assures easy shifting action and avoids slipping out of gear, which so often plagues the novice cyclist confronted with the conventional friction-loaded derailleur shift levers. Keep the attachment clamp and the little screw in the top tightened, and apply some thin lubricant to the mechanism and the point where the cable enters from time to time, and you'll get perfect shifts.

The shifting action is transmitted to the derailleurs by means of Bowden cables, named after their inventor, Frank Bowden, the founder of the British Raleigh bicycle company. The Bowden cable consists of a thin flexible steel inner cable to take tension

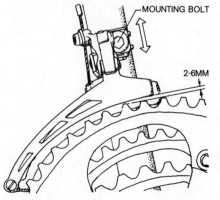

MOUNTING BOLT

2-6MM

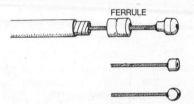

FERRULE

forces, and a hollow spiral-wound outer cable to take compressive forces. Usually the outer cable only covers part of the total inner cable, guides and tunnels serving the same purpose in other places. For mountain bike use, I recommend using fully covered cables as much as possible, since that eliminates a number of potential dirt traps.

One end of the inner cable is equipped with a soldered-on nipple. When buying a replacement, make sure the new inner cable has the nipple shape and size to fit your shift lever. The other end of the inner cable is clamped at the derailleur by means of an eye bolt or another clamping bolt. Avoid frayed ends by cutting the end off with a really sharp pair of pliers and either soldering the ends of the cable strands together, or applying epoxy cement there.

The outer cable consists of a plastic-coated steel spiral, sold by the running foot. Cut the ends off square, bending back any hook that may result, and then install a ferrule or cap over the end, so the end of the outer

The Europeans are coming: Simplex thumb shifters – look and operate just like SunTour ratchet levers.

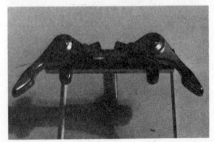

cable does not get pulled into the cable stop – you may have to remove a small piece of the plastic covering to do that. Guide the cable in such a way that it is as short as possible, consistent with smooth curves and maximum handlebar movements. Before installing the inner cable into the outer cable, apply a generous layer of grease or vaseline to the inner cable. From time to time clean and lubricate the exposed sections of inner cable.

Chainwheel and Sprocket Selection
The way most mountain bikes are set up is quite suitable for novices, who are not thoroughly familiar with using derailleur gears to their maximum advantage. In the rear, a wide-range freewheel, typically with sprockets from 14 through 26 or more teeth, is used. In the front, chainwheels almost invariably have either 24, 34, 44 or 26, 36 and 46 teeth, respectively. This provides a wide range of gears that is easy to use, since the rider can keep the chain on a particular chainwheel in the front, making almost all his gear changes with the rear derailleur only. For real off-road use, where the rider has more important things on his mind than making complicated double gear-shifts, this is an excellent arrangement.

However, if you do a high percentage of road use (and that's typical for at least ninety percent of mountain bike customers), I would recommend you consider selecting the sprockets and chainwheels more consciously. Read through the explanation in chapter 5 again and refer to Table 1 in the Appendix, if you need clarification of the terms used in the following discourse.

First consider what you want as a highest and a lowest gear. Cyclists with strong muscles, or those who aren't bent on taking on big climbs,

Typical, though not optimal, gearing with equal steps between the three chainwheels.

48-tooth outside chainwheel and a 14-tooth smallest sprocket. If you're less in a hurry, and ride on regular roads less frequently than I do, you may find 85 in more to your liking: use a 46-tooth chainwheel and a 14-tooth sprocket. Thus you have set the desired range, both in terms of gear numbers and in terms of the biggest and smallest chainwheels and sprockets. Your next job is to decide how to divide these ranges up over the 15 or so available steps of gearing.

Decide whether you can use a five-speed or a six-speed freewheel. I prefer the latter, but both the frame and the rear hub have to be designed to accommodate them (130 mm overlocknut spacing). Ideally, the percentage-steps between subsequent sprocket sizes should be about equal. The logarithmic graph overleaf allows you to do just that. Cut out a copy of detail B, align the left-hand arrow with your smallest sprocket choice, and the appropriate right-

may be satisfied with a lowest gear of around 30 in. That's low by regular road-cycling standards, but not by mountain bike standards. Feeble muscles or tough terrain may dictate you go all the way down to an 18-in bottom gear. To reach the latter, as you can tell from Table 1 in the Appendix, you'll have to use a 24-tooth chainwheel and a 34-tooth sprocket. The 30-in gear would be achieved with a 28-tooth chainwheel and a 26-tooth sprocket.

Next, consider what you want as your highest gear. I like to have a top gear of about 90 in, which I get with a

Excellent selection of chainwheel sizes: the middle chainwheel is only a little smaller than the biggest, and much bigger than the smallest. See the text for an explanation. (John Kirkpatrick / Ross Bicycles Inc. photograph)

LOWEST GEAR

HIGHEST GEAR

15-speed gearing options

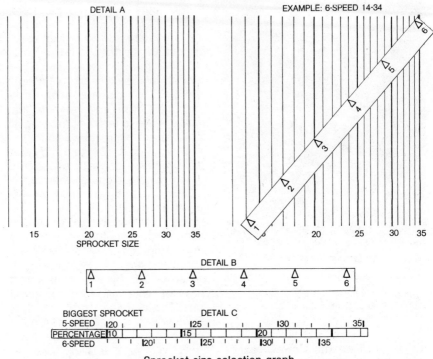

Sprocket size selection graph

hand arrow with the line corresponding with your choice of largest sprocket. Make sure you select available sizes: the smallest one may be either 13 or 14 teeth for a six-speed freewheel, only 14 for a five-speed; the largest sprocket may be either 26, 28, 30, 32 or 34 teeth. Opposite the markings 1 through 5 or 1 through 4 you can read off the most suitable intermediate sprocket sizes. Some rounding-off will be required to arrive at whole numbers, as in the example giving 14-17-20-24-28-34.

Now determine the percentage-step between each set of consecutive sprockets from detail C. The best selection of practical gears will result if you choose the two outer chainwheels in such a way, that the percentage difference between them is half as big as that between the sprockets. Our example had 20% steps, so the chainwheels should be spaced about 10% apart. Once you know the largest chainwheel and the percentage between it and the middle chainwheel, you can determine the required size for it. Our example with a 46-tooth largest chainwheel will require the middle chainwheel to have 42 teeth.

This results in a gearing system with which an intermediate gear between two subsequent rear derailleur steps can always be found by shifting the front derailleur to the other chainwheel. This applies for the entire range covered by the two outer chainwheels, in this example from 32 in to 85 in. The lower range is served entirely by the small chainwheel, covering the range from 20 in to 48 in, if a 26-tooth inner chainwheel is used.

16
The Wheels

Nothing characterizes the mountain bike more than its fat-tired wheels. Yet neither the wheel itself nor fat tires are new to the world of cycling. What is new and different, is the particular combination of dimensions and materials which makes the mountain bike's wheels as practical and efficient as they are. Their design is the secret to the unique formula for a bicycle that will go anywhere.

The bicycle wheel consists of a central hub, connected by a 'network' of spokes to a rim, on which the tire is mounted. The tire of the mountain bike consists of a separate flexible rubber or butyl inner tube and a rugged rubber-coated tire cover. In the following sections I shall describe each part in some detail, giving maintenance instructions for each.

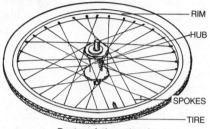

Parts of the wheel

aggressive looking tread pattern, but the allowable pressure is the real key to their success: it assures a low rolling resistance on all surfaces.

Rolling resistance is quite a significant factor in bicycling at low to moderate speeds, accounting for most of the rider's power output up to about 10 mph. On any road surface, the contact length between the tire and the road is the main factor influencing this rolling resistance. The shorter the imprint, the lower the rolling resistance. The total area of contact between the tire and the road is easy to determine, being the weight of bike and rider, divided by the

The Tire
Mountain bikes are equipped with fat tires that differ from old-fashioned fat tires in allowing a high inflation pressure. They also have a more

An interesting set of (small) wheels on this backyard special. More typically, mountain bikes have 26-in wheels. Note that the front wheel is radially spoked. (David Epperson/BICYCLE SPORT photograph)

tire pressure. If bike and rider weigh a total of 200 lbs, the total imprint of two tires inflated to 20 psi will be 10 sq in; if the tires are inflated to 100 psi, the imprint will be only 2 sq in. Dividing this area by the width of the imprint gives its length: if it's 2 in wide, the imprint length will be 5 in in the first case, and in the case of the higher pressure it will only be 1 in long, resulting in a similarly reduced value for the rolling resistance.

It's not simply a matter of inflating any old tire to a higher value, since the tire has to be designed to take the pressure. It is easiest to construct tires that will take a high pressure by making them small in cross section. That, in addition to the resulting lower weight, explains why racing bikes have skinny tires. It should be pointed out that a racing bike with skinny tires is not efficient on account of the tire's narrowness, but on account of the resulting pressure increase and the weight reduction. Underinflated skinny tires are no more efficient than fat tires operating at the same pressure.

On soft surfaces the tire pressure is less of a determinant for the contact length between tire and ground, since the ground deforms, rather than the tire. Under those conditions the tire width is the major determinant: the wider tire sinks in less than the skinny one. On rough surfaces both factors play a role, as well as a third factor, tire flexibility – the more

flexible tire wastes less power. This latter factor is a function of tire construction and weight.

Only in recent years have tires come on the market that are constructed so as to provide an optimum balance for riding on mixed terrain. These are the modern fat tires, which are relatively light and flexible in their construction, yet accept pressures of up to 90 psi. Besides, they are highly resistant to punctures, and have enough of a profile to give a firm grip on all surfaces.

Practically all these tires are designed to fit a rim size that corresponds to the old steel rim found on the American utility bicycle, namely with a rim shoulder diameter of 559 mm. New aluminum alloy rims have been introduced which are both stronger and lighter, but they almost all have this critical dimension in common.

Tire size designation is a bit of a mess in the US and Japan, although the Europeans have had a simpler and more sensible system for years. This sensible system, known as ETRTO-standard, designates both the tire and the rim by the rim shoulder diameter and the width – tires by their inflated width in mm, rims by their outside width in mm. The critical dimension is the rim shoulder diameter, and is the earlier mentioned size of 559mm for all nominal 26-in mountain bike tires. This is important, because there are also 26-in tires that fit only other rim sizes, e.g. the French and English balloon tires, which fit 584mm and 571mm rims respectively.

Within reason, any width of rim will fit your tires, as long as it has the right rim shoulder diameter. In fact, narrower rims have the advantage of leaving more of the tire protruding. This gives them a more nearly circular cross section, which results in more

HARD ROAD   SOFT GROUND

HIGH PRESS.

LOW PRESS.

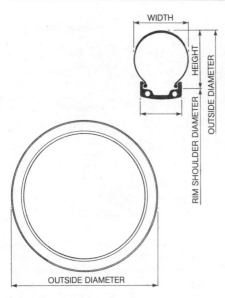

Tire sizing

install 24-in tires with 507 mm rims on the smallest frame sizes. Note that the 26-in and 650 x 35 B wheels are not interchangeable, since the brakes are set for a certain rim size.

There are quite a few brands of mountain bike tires, and even more different tread profiles. Choosing one of them is more a declaration of faith than a rational act. I suggest you try my flexibility test, as described above, and select a profile which you think will do the job. Try another type next time if you're not happy.

Weights vary quite a bit, namely from 750 to 1050 gm for 26 x 2.125 tires. The heavier tire does not necessarily last longer, and it certainly does require more power to accelerate.

One unique tire is made by the Finnish Nokia company: it comes in a studded version for use on ice and snow, called Stud Haka. These studs may even be removed and reinstalled next winter. The British mountain bike builders Cleland mount these tires on their Range Rider. Studded tires are to my knowledge not (yet) available in a size to fit the 559 mm rim of most mountain bikes. I know of two models, 40 and 50 mm wide respectively, to fit the 584 mm rims for 650 x 35 B tires, as well as skinnier tires to fit 622 mm and 630 mm rims for 700C and 27-in wheels on regular ten-speeds.

The tube is generally made of butyl, although lighter tubes of latex (i.e. unvulcanized rubber) are also available. The latter are more flexible and generally lose air a lot faster,

flexibility and more comfort on rough surfaces. The other characteristic that improves these two properties of a tire is found in two construction details: non-rubberized sidewalls and great overall flexibility due to correct construction of the tire's carcass. This latter detail is most readily recognizable by trying to stretch the tire between two hands, as illustrated below.

The most common tire sizes for mountain bikes are nominally designated 26 x 2.125 and 26 x 1.75. Both fit 559 mm rims and should probably be designated 57-559 and 47-559 respectively in the ETRTO-system. Recently some mountain bikes intended more for road use than for off-road applications have been equipped with narrower tires, designated by the old French marking 650 x 35 B. These latter tires do not fit standard 559 mm rims: they are designed for 584 mm rims, and their ETRTO designation is 40-584 or 37-584, depending on their actual cross section. Some manufacturers

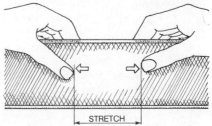

which makes them the choice for racing, but not for everyday riding. Specially coated latex tubes (e.g. Sup-Air or Imp-Air trade names) keep the air in longer, but there is a trick to be aware of. With regular rubber or butyl tubes it is fine to use a narrower tube, made for 26 x 1.75 tires, even on the wider 26 x 2.125 tires, since the tube is flexible enough. However, the coating on the air-sealed latex tubes does not stand up to that much stretch: use only the corresponding size tube and tire, otherwise it'll lose air anyway. Butyl tubes are not less puncture-prone than the light latex tubes, except the extra thick thorn-proof butyl tube: use it where thorns are the problem.

Most tubes for mountain bikes are equipped with the conventional Schraeder valve, also used on car tires. It is a poor choice for bicycle use, since it contains a spring closure, which 'swallows' too much of the pumping pressure to allow adequate inflation with a hand pump. And there are no gas stations on the trail... Make sure you get tubes with the so-called Presta valves, as used on racing tires, and get a pump to match.

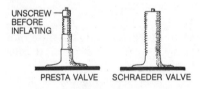

UNSCREW BEFORE INFLATING

PRESTA VALVE   SCHRAEDER VALVE

Valve types

Tire Maintenance

Even if you never learn to do anything else yourself, as a bicyclist you just have to know how to fix a flat. Here's how you go about it:

1. Check to see whether the source is visible from the outside; if so, mark its location and remove it.

2. Either place the bike upside-down or remove the wheel from the

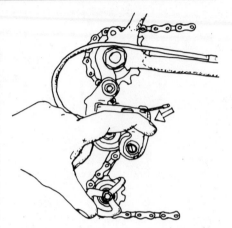

bike. To remove a rear wheel, put the chain on the smallest sprocket and hold the derailleur back. If you put the bike upside-down, support it in such a way that the gear shifters and the cables don't get damaged.

3. Let out any remaining air at the valve; unscrew and remove the lock-nut.

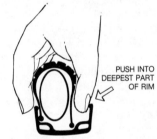

PUSH INTO DEEPEST PART OF RIM

4. Push the bead of the tire on one side into the deeper center of the rim, working all around both sides of the valve.

5. Place one of the three tire irons (bought in the bike shop, together with the patch kit) under the bead which you have just worked towards the center of the rim; lift the bead over the edge of the rim and hook the tire iron on a spoke.

6. Do the same five or six inches over, using the second tire iron.

7. And with the third. Now the middle tire iron will fall out – you may

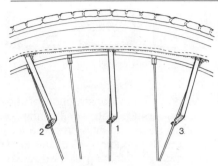

use it as a fourth, if necessary.

8. Work the entire bead over the edge of the rim with your bare hand, working around.

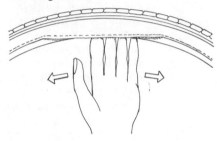

9. Starting at the valve, bring the inner tube outside the tire cover.

10. Inflate the tire (on a Presta valve the end screw must be loosened first) and listen for escaping air. If necessary, submerge in water and watch for bubbles of escaping air; dry the tire afterwards. Mark the location of the hole.

11. Choose an appropriately sized patch and use sandpaper to roughen an area of the tube around the hole, a little bigger than the patch, after which you wipe that area clean.

12. Apply a thin layer of rubber solution from the patch kit over an area slightly bigger than the patch.

13. Let dry about three minutes; remove the foil or cloth protector from the adhesive side of the patch and apply it firmly, making sure it is positioned properly before you do, since it can't be moved again.

14. If you have talcum powder, sprinkle some over the area, so the tube does not subsequently stick to the inside of the tire cover.

15. Inflate the tube to check if it's alright now; repair again if necessary.

16. Check the inside of the tire cover and remove any foreign objects. Particularly tricky are thorns, which you can only find by compressing the tire tread.

17. Check whether any of the spokes are protruding from the heads of the nipples; if so, file smooth. Cover all the spokes with the protective rim tape.

18. Any holes or tears in the tire cover may be mended similarly, using a piece of discarded regular (skinny) bicycle tire, which you'll stick to the inside of the tire cover with rubber solution on both the patch and the inside of the tire cover.

19. Insert the valve through the valve hole and inflate the tire slightly, then work it back over the rim under the tire cover.

20. Let most of the air out again, and start working the bead of cover back over the edge of the rim, starting opposite the valve and working in both directions until only the area near the valve remains outside.

21. Release all remaining air, push the bead into the deeper center of the rim, and pull the remaining section of the bead over the edge with your bare hands (use tire irons only to *remove*, never to *install* the tire).

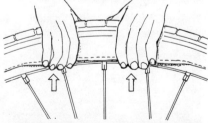

22. Inflate the tire slightly, then squeeze the tire all around to make sure the tube is not caught anywhere and that the tire is centered cor-

rectly: the distance between the edge of the rim and the concentric marking around the side of the tire should be the same on both sides around the entire circumference.

23. Install the valve locknut, and inflate the tire to its final pressure: 80 to 90 psi for smooth roads, 50 to 60 for rougher terrain, only 30 to 40 psi for soft ground. In each case the heavily loaded rear wheel should be inflated about 5 psi more than the less loaded front wheel. To reinstall the wheel, you may have to loosen the brake (see chapter 17).

When replacing either the tire or the tube, proceed just as described above for removal and installation of the tire and tube. Always make sure the tire has the right size for the rim. You may use a narrower tube for a thicker tire, but not the other way round. Even within a certain designation, actual inflated tire widths vary quite a bit, so if there is relatively little clearance between the tire and the chain stays, be sure not to get a model that is even fatter. Use only tubes with Presta valves, and inspect the condition of the rim tape – replace by one or two layers of cotton handlebar tape, as used on the dropped handlebars for ten-speed bikes, if the original tape is damaged.

Cross section of aluminum alloy rim with hollow ribs. The ridges in the sides of the rim are intended to improve wet braking.

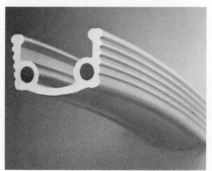

Rim section types

The Rim

The design and construction of the rim has contributed significantly to the progress with high-pressure fat-tire wheels. Modern rims of this kind are made of aluminum alloy and have one of the cross section patterns illustrated. Within each type there are stronger and weaker models, and I can express no preference. But if you care about relative weights and prices, the model with the hollow double bottom, referred to as 'box section', tends to be the lightest and most expensive, whereas the model with the solid ribs is the heaviest and cheapest of the lot. People who express strong preferences tend to agree that the Japanese makes Ukai and Araya are the strongest rims available.

HOOK EDGE RIM

STRAIGHT SIDE RIM

Tire seating systems

The rim sizing problem was already discussed in the section about tires. In short, the rim shoulder diameter is the critical dimension; it is most easily checked by wrapping a rope or a tape around the rim shoulder and dividing its length by 3.14. The appropriate dimension for 26 x 2.125 and 26 x 1.75 tires, as well as for the 'intermediate' size 26 x 2.10, is 559 mm. The correct size for 650 x 35 B tires is 584 mm, whereas smaller bikes with 24-in wheels should have rims with a rim shoulder diameter of 507 mm.

The width is less critical: anything in excess of about 22 mm, measured externally, will be wide enough to hold any mountain bike tire. One interesting way of arriving at a light rim and a flexible round tire cross section was pioneered by frame builder Ross Schaeffer of Santa Cruz. Schaeffer starts out with a standard 630 mm rim, as used for skinny 27-in tires, removes a four-spoke section, and bends the rim back into shape. The result is a wheel with 32 spokes (which is not my idea of an improvement) of narrow cross section, which is good, since it makes the tire more flexible. I suppose rim manufacturers will not lose much time copying Schaeffer's solution, except that they'll drill the rim with the standard number of 36 spoke holes.

As concerns maintenance, rims sometimes take a lot of abuse, leading to dents and warps. The stronger the rim, the less likely this is to happen, and the harder it will be to correct a problem like that. You may leave this work to a bicycle mechanic. If the wheel is merely out of round, it will appear to be wobbling as you look from behind when turning the wheel. This problem can usually be corrected by means of loosening and tightening certain spokes. The entire wheel must be re-spoked if either the rim or the hub is to be replaced. Both operations will be described under *Wheel Maintenance* below.

The Hub

The illustration shows a typical hub, as used on most mountain bikes. It has adjustable bearings, which are protected by means of a plastic seal to keep out dirt and water. The area between the bearing-cup and the cone, where the bearing balls lie, is filled with grease. To adjust the bearings, loosen the locknut, lift the lock washer, and turn the cone in or out, after which the cone is held fixed, while you tighten the locknut again.

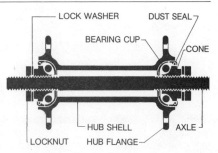

Some of the more expensive hubs have cartridge bearings, as generally used in industrial machinery. Most people refer to those items as 'sealed-bearing hubs'. However, adjustable bearings may also have seals, and are not necessarily inferior. Cartridge bearing hubs are not adjustable: when they have developed slack, the bearings must be replaced.

The hub of the mountain bike wheel is not held in the frame by means of a quick-release, as it is on the ten-speed, but by means of axle nuts, often with integral washers. This allows the use of a stronger solid axle, and doesn't offer the risk of accidental loosening. There is some misunderstanding about the relative strengths of hollow and solid axles. For the same weight, hollow axles

Typical medium quality off-road hub with adjustable bearings from Shimano.

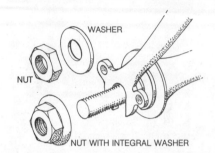

WASHER

NUT

NUT WITH INTEGRAL WASHER

can be made slightly stronger against bending forces than solid axles by using a greater outside diameter. However, given a particular material, solid axles are always stronger (as well as heavier and cheaper) than hollow axles of the same diameter. So the solid axles for mountain bike hubs are stronger since they have the same big diameter as hollow axles.

From time to time your hubs should be adjusted, lubricated and overhauled. To do the latter job, which includes the other two as well, proceed as follows:

1. Remove the wheel from the bike. On the rear wheel make sure the chain is on the smallest sprocket, and hold back the chain and the derailleur.

2. Remove the axle nut on one end. On the other end you may screw the axle nut tightly up to the locknut, to maintain its position.

3. Remove the locknut on the free end, using a wrench, while countering the underlying cone with a special cone wrench (bought in the bicycle shop – it's a very thin open-ended wrench).

4. Remove the lock washer and the cone, catching the bearing balls in a rag.

5. Pull the axle out towards the

opposite side, again catching the bearing balls.

6. Clean and inspect all parts. Discard anything damaged, bent, pitted or grooved; always replace the bearing balls.

7. Fill the bearing-cups with bearing grease and insert the bearing balls; then reassemble in reverse order.

8. To adjust: loosen the locknut, countering against the cone on the same side; loosen or tighten the cone: against the *cone* on the other side when loosening, against the *locknut* on the other side when tightening. Tighten the locknut against the cone on the same side.

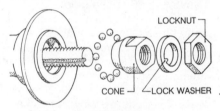

LOCKNUT

CONE   LOCK WASHER

The Spokes

The illustration shows the spoke and its nipple, as well as the way its length is determined: from the *inside* of the bend. Most wheels have 36 spokes, laced together in a regular pattern. You will notice upon examination of a wheel that the pattern repeats itself every fourth spoke. Out of the 36 spokes, nine go to the outside of the left-hand hub flange, nine go to the inside of the same hub flange, nine to the outside of the right-hand hub flange, and the remaining nine go to the inside of that same flange. On their way from the hub to the rim the spokes cross one another in a regular pattern. The rear wheel is spoked asymmetrically to center the rim between the hub locknuts.

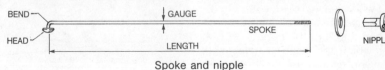

BEND

HEAD

GAUGE

SPOKE

LENGTH

NIPPLE

Spoke and nipple

I shall not bore you here with the relative merits of the various spoking patterns. If you ever want to rebuild a wheel, the easiest way is to tape the new rim on top of the old rim, making sure the valve holes are in line. Then remove the spokes one-by-one, each time installing it in the corresponding hole in the new rim.

If you want to replace the spokes themselves, things get more complicated. However, if you remember that the pattern repeats itself every fourth spoke, and if you tackle only nine spokes at a time, you'll find your way out of the apparent maze without detailed instructions. Make sure you get the right length (measured in mm) and the right thickness

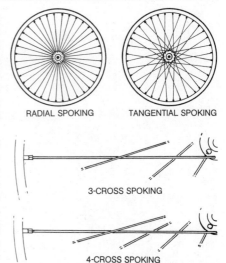

RADIAL SPOKING   TANGENTIAL SPOKING

3-CROSS SPOKING

4-CROSS SPOKING

of spokes. For mountain bike use I prefer stainless steel spokes with a thickness of 2.3 mm (13 gauge) – I've seen even thicker ones. The holes in the hub and the rim may have to be drilled out to accept these thicker spokes.

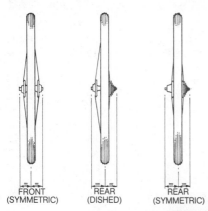

FRONT
(SYMMETRIC)   REAR
(DISHED)   REAR
(SYMMETRIC)

Wheel Maintenance
In addition to the work on the tires and the hub, covered in preceding sections of this chapter, the most frequent wheel maintenance job is straightening out a warped or buckled wheel. If the problem is really dra-

Special rear hub with built-in brake, made by Sturmey-Archer. There is a matching hub for the front. See my comments about hub brakes in chapter 17.

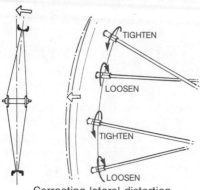

Correcting lateral distortion

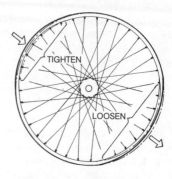

Correcting radial distortion

matic, you will be best advised to find someone who does this kind of thing for a living. However, the kind of buckle that makes your brake ineffective or merely causes vibrations or imprecise handling can usually be alleviated by means of tightening and loosening certain numbers of spokes. All you need is a spoke wrench for the appropriate spoke size (bought in any bike shop). Turn the bike upside-down, protecting the gear shift levers, and proceed as follows:

1. Determine what is the nature of your particular wheel problem by comparing with the two illustrations.

2. Slowly turn the wheel to determine where the offending section is located, and in which direction the deviation from the correct plane is: up or down in the one case, left or

right in the other. Mark the side of the tire with chalk to reflect this.

3. In the case of radial deviation, loosen the spokes in the 'flat spot', and tighten the other spokes a little. Check and, if necessary, repeat.

4. In the case of lateral deviation, loosen the spokes on the side of the projection, and tighten them on the opposite side in that same area. In each case only turn the nipples one half to one turn at a time, rechecking and correcting frequently.

Individual broken spokes should be replaced as soon as possible. Spokes usually break at the head, sometimes at the nipple, but never in between. As soon as a spoke breaks, remove it from the wheel, so it does not get caught in the moving parts of the bike. Use the old spoke as a reference to get the correct spoke length and thickness for replacement. Buy a few extra spokes as spares. Sometimes you will have to straighten out the entire wheel according to the preceding description when a broken spoke has been replaced. You'll need a spoke wrench either way.

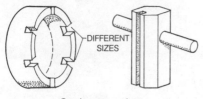

Spoke wrenches

17
The Brakes

Consider what happens when you come rolling down a hill on your mountain bike, heading straight for a giant sequoia, or whatever else is cluttering the backwoods in your part of the world. You have three choices: run into the obstacle, ride around it, or stop before you get there. For the first option you need a helmet, a new bike and some luck; both of the other options require the use of a reliable brake. If there's no room to divert, but enough to stop, you may pull the brakes and stop in time. Usually, however, you will merely use the brakes to slow down to such a speed that you can safely handle diverting maneuvers.

Technically seen, what you are doing, whether just slowing down or grinding to a halt, is similar. There's a lot of kinetic energy stored up in the moving bicycle – a function of speed and mass. With your brakes you try to dissipate either all or some of that energy: in the first instance to stop dead, in the second to get down to a lower speed. If you hit the tree, you'll also dissipate all the energy stored up in the bicycle, with disastrous effect...

In practice, it is worthwhile to distinguish between two basic forms of braking: to regulate speed on a downhill, and to stop dead. Oddly enough, the speed regulation is usually the more demanding, since it is generally not just done to escape one particular tree, but to keep the speed down within the range at which you can control the bike over a longer period. In that case you'll be dissipating the bicycle's energy as it is being generated by the downslope during quite a long time. What hap-pens while you're applying the brake is simple too: the excess kinetic energy is transformed into another form of energy, namely heat.

The amount of heat generated while braking on a long steep slope is quite substantial. The predecessor of the modern mountain bike was equipped with a coaster brake in the rear wheel only. If you take a look at a coaster brake and consult an old high school physics text, you will appreciate what's wrong with that solution. To dissipate heat you require a large conducting cooling area, and the coaster brake's cooling area consists of nothing but the hub shell, which is tiny.

Rim brakes, by contrast, work on the large cooling area of the wheel

Very attractive and rigid cantilever brakes from Shimano.

rim. If you get further into the physics book, you may accuse me of oversimplifying the situation. The book will tell you that a smaller area will do fine if you run it to a higher temperature and get plenty of air to blow past it. The problem with all hub brakes is that they can't be run at very high temperatures, since that would damage the wheel bearings. Similarly, the rim brake shouldn't be operated too hot, to prevent damage to the tires, a problem not encountered under off-road conditions, but familiar to tandem riders. One type of brake is suitable for very high operating temperatures, namely the disc brake, which is indeed used on some mountain bikes. But for all practical purposes, the rim brake can be considered standard equipment on virtually all mountain bikes.

However, I feel that for areas with more rain, mud and slush, and fewer precipitous descents, other types of brakes should be seriously considered. Mud and snow build up quickly at rim brakes, and moisture on the rims acts like a lubricant, reducing the effectiveness of the rim brake significantly when wet. Although all mountain bikes worth their name are equipped with aluminum rims, which suffer far less from the effects of moisture on the rim than steel ver-

sions, wet braking will always remain a problem as long as rim brakes are used.

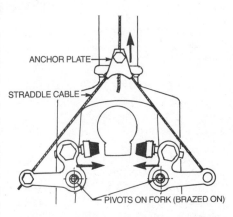

Cantilever Brakes

The type of rim brake universally used on mountain bikes is the cantilever brake, which is also the standard on cyclo-cross machines and tandems. As compared to the various kinds of calliper brakes used on conventional ten-speed bicycles, the cantilever brake has the advantage of fixed pivots, mounted close to the braking point. This results in less distortion of the brake arms, which would be excessive in the case of calliper brakes designed to reach all the way around the mountain bike's fat tires and generous clearances.

You will notice that I am not claiming inherently more braking power for the cantilever brake than for the calliper brake. Anybody who does that admits to not understanding the elementary physical principles behind braking. The effectiveness of any brake is determined by two factors: the braking force, and the coefficient of friction between the brake pad and the braking surface (i.e. the rim). The coefficient of friction remains the same, given the same rim and brake shoe materials. The force is determined by the total lever-

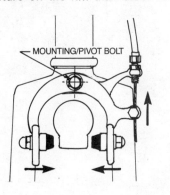

Calliper brake (sidepull)

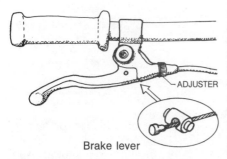

Brake lever

age (confusingly referred to as *mechanical advantage*) between the applicator and the brake shoe, and the application force, subtracting friction losses in the control mechanism.

Inherently there is no difference between the two systems, calliper brake and cantilever brake. Levers, linkages and controls can be (and frequently are) designed so that the same mechanical advantage or leverage is achieved in either case. In fact, you may not want too much leverage, since that would require more lever travel, for which many people's hands just aren't big enough. The sole advantages of cantilever brakes in this particular application are their shape, which makes them act less as dirt traps in muddy terrain, and the fact that their brake arms are so short as to remain rigid, assuring accurately controlled braking without undue vibrations. To make a calliper brake equally rigid would require a much heavier construction, to counter the greater flexibility of its longer brake arms.

The French Mafac brake, which is no longer made, though many suppliers have a sizable stock of them, is the granddaddy of cantilever brakes. Several manufacturers now offer brakes based on this design. Each should be mounted on special bosses, brazed to the fork blades and the seat stays. However, interchangeability is usually possible. They all work quite similarly, the braking effectiveness appearing to be less dependent on the design of the brake than on the quality of the levers and the cables. Shimano's brake is certainly the prettiest and, if anything, the most rigid of the lot. For best operation, all cantilever brakes should be installed under a slight angle, so the front portion of the brake shoe touches the rim first. Adjustment of this variable and the position of the brake shoe is usually provided.

Brake Controls

The mountain bike's cantilever brakes are controlled from the levers on the handlebars by means of Bowden cables, similar to the ones described in chapter 15, *Gearing Mechanisms*. To take the significantly higher forces, brake inner cables should be thicker than those used for the derailleurs. The result of using

Cam-operated off-road brake designed by Charles Cunningham – now available from SunTour.

thin cables is a spungy feel of the brakes, whereby the cables seem to 'give', rather than delivering full braking force.

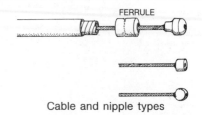

Cable and nipple types

Some of the spunginess of inadequate mountain bike brake controls is attributable to insufficient rigidity of the brake levers, and there's nothing you can do about that, short of replacing them by a heavier type. But it is still worthwhile to make sure the inner cables are at least 2.0 mm. Select an outer cable that does not 'give' (i.e. get shorter) when compressed, and has the right diameter to match the inner cable: the two must be free to move relative to each other with minimal friction. Particularly nice are special PTFE-lined outer cables.

As in the case of derailleur controls, the inner cable should be lubricated generously before it is put through the outer cable. Place fitting ferrules on the ends of the sections of outer cable where they enter fixed attachments on the frame and on the brake levers; you may have to remove a short piece of the outer cable's plastic coating to make them fit.

The brake levers used on mountain bikes are similar in design to those used on light motorcycles. The most popular ones are those made by Shimano, Dia-Compe and Tomasselli. Since the former two manufacturers make their own cantilever brakes, you will usually find the Tomasselli levers only on bikes equipped with brakes of other brands. These are genuine motorcycle levers and are an excellent choice, as are the Dia-Compe levers, which are quite similar. Shimano levers and cables are less rigid, although the matching brake is a real beauty. As with so many other parts, I would shy away from unbranded brakes and levers used on some of the cheapest mountain bikes: I've seen several broken brake levers in that category.

Always install the brake lever under such an angle that it is readily at hand, without having to first move the position of the hand or twist the wrist. To avoid corrosive deterioration of the cable near the nipple, put some grease in that area and cover

Roller-cam brake for the rear wheel. It is mounted under the chain stays, instead of on the seat stays. This leads to less cable friction and more rigidity.

up the gap in the lever through which the cable is visible with a piece of adhesive tape. This is one of the tips you learn by talking to motorcyclists, which can be very educational for any mountain bike rider. If your brake lever gets bent in a spill, you should be able to bend it back into shape. Check to make sure it has no cracks.

Other Brakes
Although virtually all commercially built mountain bikes worthy of their name use cantilever brakes, some small manufacturers choose a different route. Without getting into much detail, I'd like to mention these briefly. One interesting brake is the cam-operated brake designed by California frame builder Charles Cunningham, which is somewhat akin to the Shimano Parapull brake. This brake is now available from SunTour; it works very smoothly and reliably. Weinmann's new HP Turbo spindle-operated brake requires special braze-ons; it's still too soon to judge its quality.

Several manufacturers use some kind of hub brake or disc brake. The commercially available brakes of this type don't seem to stand up to mountain bike use, but the models installed by reputable frame builders have generally been built or modified to take the abuse. The Shimano disc brake has been installed on special hubs (because the matching Shimano hub is not suitable for our kind of use), most successfully in the rear. Cleland of England installs very fine drum brakes of their own manufacture on both wheels. Maxicar, Araya and Swallow drum brakes also seem an excellent choice.

In general, I would shy away from brakes which act near the center of the front wheel, as both the disc brake and the hub brake do. I feel that their action at the tip of the fork might tend to bend or damage the fork when applied hard on a steep descent. I may be proven wrong in this, and I would certainly recommend their use in relatively level terrain, especially if the local problem is rain, because hub brakes and disc brakes work quite well under the kind of weather conditions where the rim brake does not.

Brake Maintenance
The most frequently required form of brake maintenance is adjustment of the controls, to compensate for brake shoe wear and apparent stretch of the control cables. Before adjusting, check to make sure the rims are dry and clean, and that the cables are operating freely. Replace damaged or pinched sections of outer cable or an inner cable with

Sturmey-Archer hub brake for the front wheel. See the text for my reservations.

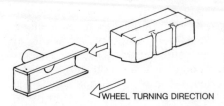

WHEEL TURNING DIRECTION

broken strands. Lubricate the cable as well as the pivots at the brake and the lever. Replace either just the brake block or the entire brake shoe if it is worn very far, making sure brake shoes with one open end are installed as shown in the illustration, so they will not be pushed out by the movement of the wheel. Now proceed as follows:

1. Pull the lever and verify whether the brake shoe touches the rim over its entire length and width. Adjust by means of the brake-shoe attachment bolt, if necessary.

2. Let go of the lever and check wether the wheel is free to turn without scraping the brake, and whether both brake shoes retract equally

far. You may have to straighten the wheel (per chapter 16), as well as correcting the position of the brake shoe in the brake arm.

3. Pull the lever again, and establish whether the brake stops the bike powerfully enough with at least 2 cm (¾in) between the lever and the handlebars. Adjust by means of the barrel adjuster on the brake lever, or by moving the cable end where it is clamped in the eye bolt (at the point where the brake cable picks up the little straddle cable which connects the two brake arms). To do that, first clamp the brake arms together, so you can unhook one end of the straddle cable. Reinstall the straddle cable after adjusting.

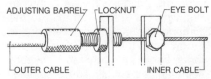

ADJUSTING BARREL — LOCKNUT — EYE BOLT — OUTER CABLE — INNER CABLE

4. Check operation and clearance again, then adjust the other brake, following the same procedure. Try out the brakes separately while riding at walking speed. The front brake should lock so the rear wheel begins to lift off – release immediately. The rear brake should lock and skid.

To remove or install a wheel, you will often have to release the brake, since the fat tires don't fit past the brake shoes as easily as they do on most regular bicycles. To do that, squeeze the brake shoes together with one hand, and unhook the nipple

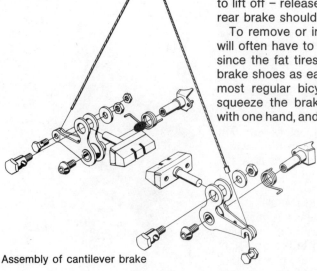

Assembly of cantilever brake

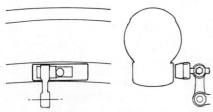

Brake shoe adjustment

at the end of the straddle cable with the other. Now you can pivot the brakes out to clear the wheel. Check for proper alignment and adjustment of the brake after reinstalling the wheel, and make sure the brake return spring has not slipped off its end stop, causing the brake arm to just 'dangle', as may happen on some models.

Finally a piece of preventative maintenance or accident prevention technique. Some cyclists report losing the straddle cable, either due to a loose anchor bolt or due to the cable or its anchor plate breaking. If that happens in the front, the straddle cable may be picked up by the tire and jam up the wheel when it

comes around again. It has been suggested to tie the straddle cable loosely to a fixed part of the bike, using a generous loop of twine or a shoe lace. I don't bother, but you may consider it worth the trouble.

Symmetric calliper brake from Scott-Matthauser. This very rigid construction might even be suitable for off-road use, if it were made in the appropriate size. (Darryl Skrabak photograph)

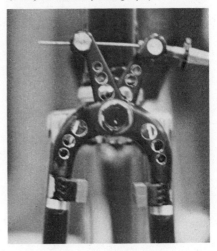

18
Accessories

You can mount a lot of gadgets on a bicycle, some useful, some not. I probably don't need to warn you about the risk of installing too many useful accessories, since Americans are by nature suspicious of anything that might add to the utility of the bicycle. Where else would one see nearly all cyclists on machines without fenders, without lights, without luggage racks? In other societies, more used to thinking about the bicycle as a useful device, all those items are standard equipment, as are lock, bell and chainguard.

I've grown accustomed to seeing bicycles that lack all utilitarian amenities. But I also know better, so I

Special off-road fenders from Madison of Great Britain.

may be in a good position to advise you on the selection of additional equipment. The mountain bike is a practical device, which in its very essence appeals to man's sense of reason and proportion. Assuming some of these sensible streaks are also present in the souls of people who choose to ride such bicycles, I think we have a good basis to equip your machine so it is more practical.

Not all the equipment described here must always be mounted on the bike, if only because some of it may get vandalized. For that reason, I would say a sizeable bag that can be used both on and off the bike is one of your best investments: put your removable accessories in the bag and take it with you whenever you leave the bike. Use either a big English type saddlebag or a separate bag that is carried on top of a luggage rack, if you choose to install a rack. At a pinch, a large handlebar bag may serve the same purpose; it probably works better on a mountain bike than on a regular ten-speed. Attach a long carrying strap with which you can carry it like a shoulder bag off the bike.

Many accessories can be selected or modified to make them easily installed and removed to suit your trip purposes. Of course, bags, pumps and water bottles are designed to be removable. But also other parts can be adapted: use wingnuts and wing screws to mount racks, reflectors, and fenders. You can easily make your own wing screws by soldering a sizable washer in the screwdriver slot of a screw. You can either leave this job to the bicycle mechanic or get any high school

SOLDER WASHER IN SLOT

Home-made wing bolt

metal working class to do it for you, if you don't have the equipment to do it yourself.

Luggage Racks

Some manufacturers make special racks to fit mountain bikes, and most mountain bike manufacturers are kind enough to install brazed-on bosses on their frames to match those racks. If no braze-ons are provided, you may have to rely on clamps, installed around the stays, fork blades or frame tubes, to support the racks. To stop these clamps from shifting, I suggest you first stick a rubber tire-patch around the tube in the appropriate location.

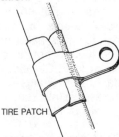

TIRE PATCH

Learn to judge the rigidity of a luggage rack, to make sure you don't finish up with a rack that swings and vibrates, leading to unpredictable handling of the bike. There must be fixed mounting points at the top near the seat stays (rear rack) or the fork crown (front rack), as well as at least two pairs of more or less vertical supports, one pair of which should be sloping inward, to act as a lateral brace. The front rack should be designed similar to the Blackburn Low Rider rack, on which the front bags hang well below the top of the front wheel. It has been demonstrat-

ed that this is the mounting position which least interferes with the handling characteristics of the bicycle.

Attaching bags to the racks is also an art and a science. Make sure they are attached so they can not sway either back and forth or sideways. This is achieved by attaching the bottom of the bags as well as the top. The most reliable attachment is by means of leather or webbing straps with sturdy buckles. Bungee-cords, though popular, are quite unsuitable for any purpose except tying the bottom of a handlebar bag down to the fork-ends. Watch out that you don't get the end of a bungee-cord hooked on a spoke: it will allow you to ride quite a ways, and then suddenly block your wheel...

To keep the weight of racks reasonably low, aluminum alloy is generally used. Tubular steel is also a very nice material for this application, and is less likely to break than many cheaper welded aluminum racks. From time to time some crazy manufacturer comes out with a plastic rack; I haven't seen a good one yet.

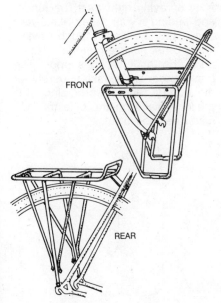

FRONT

REAR

Fenders

Until recently, fenders to fit around the mountain bike's fat tires were just not available. However, several excellent fenders are now available. The plastic Bluemels and ESGE models are attached with stays (which unfortunately are too close to the tires, to satisfy another unreasonable CPSC regulation, thought they can be modified). The British Madison fenders are perhaps more interesting for most cyclists, since they are easily removable.

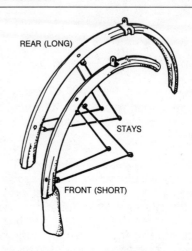

REAR (LONG)
STAYS
FRONT (SHORT)

The attachment stays for fenders should preferably be run over the top of the fenders, so they don't form a mud trap between the fender and the tire. If you want the advantages of fenders and are not able to find any, you can make your own. I've seen beautiful hand-made fenders of plexiglass, a material that is easy to bend at moderate temperatures. Sandblasting them on the inside gives them an attractive appearance.

At the bottom of every respectable front fender there is a mud flap, which helps to keep water and slush from spraying right past the fender and landing in your shoes. Make your own, using a sheet of tough vinyl or some other flexible material, attached to the fender or its support. The back fender lends itself superbly for mounting a rear reflector, since it is the one place on the bike that will never get obscured.

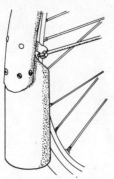

On the right-hand side of the rear wheel a lot of dirt and mud is thrown off onto the chain and the front chainwheel. It seems a good idea for those who ride in rain, mud and snow to install a guard there, between the front portion of the wheel and the chain, attaching it to the fender. Plexiglass seems a pretty good material for this handiman-project too. The idea is not as crazy as it sounds: at least Cleland, the British manufacturer of Range Rider mountain bikes, installs such a guard (though not of plexiglass).

Lighting Equipment

It is virtually impossible to install enough lighting equipment on a mountain bike to be able to do off-road cycling at night, except on a lit-up ski slope or when it's a full moon. The following recommendations are therefore not so much intended to make nighttime off-road cycling possible or safe, as to get you home on the regular road safely. Your lighting equipment should both make you visible to others who could endanger you (or whom you might endanger), and it should help you see obstacles and dangers on the road ahead of you.

Lighting equipment is not only needed when it is really dark, but also at dusk and in the fog. If you have at all driven a car under such conditions, you will almost certainly remember hairy situations with cyclists appearing out of nowhere. You eventually only saw those cyclists because your own headlights were aimed at them. That goes both for cyclists with and without the legally prescribed reflectors, with which bikes must be equipped when sold in the US. Keep in mind: reflectors are only visible to those whose own headlights are shining upon them.

If you are riding a bicycle, even with lights, you will not have the kind of illuminating potential the motorist has. As a result, you will rarely throw enough of your light onto someone else's reflector to make him visible to you. At dusk and in the fog, when quite a few motorists drive without lights, or when their lights do not penetrate very far, reflectors are not totally effective either.

Dangers of nighttime collisions can be divided into two categories: those in front and those behind. In front includes those coming from the side, ahead of the cyclist; behind means those who are in a position to overtake or hit you from behind. Of the dangers ahead, by far the most imminent are those coming out of a side street, since they will be crossing your path. Of the ones behind, none will be anywhere except straight behind you before they become a danger to you.

To appease those who endanger you from behind, a good rear reflector, mounted in the back and reflecting straight behind you, is therefore fully adequate, except when other road users don't use lights or in a thick fog. Those who endanger you from the front generally can not benefit from your front reflector, since most of the ones who cross your path (about 90 percent, to give you an idea of the magnitude) are still in a side street, with their headlights aimed elsewhere than upon your front reflector. To protect you against dangers in front of you, only a headlight is any use at all!

Of the remaining reflectors in the prescribed package, the ones on the spokes serve no useful purpose at all, since the motorist who will hit you from the side is still ahead of you, with his headlights shining where you will be later. If he *is* a danger to you he can't slow down in time. Pedal reflectors are o.k. as a mediocre substitute for a really big rear reflector: though their movement and their light amber color make them more readily visible, they are too small.

Reflector, rear light and the world's most comfortable saddle.

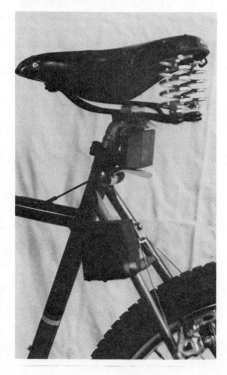

The CPSC-prescribed front and rear reflectors are all designed with astonishing ignorance of the accident generating phenomena and the physical and optical laws which govern reflector design. Being divided into three areas, each responding only to light from a certain direction, only one third will ever reflect the headlights of the motorist who might hit you: the center section, which faces straight back. But this is only a third as big as it could be if the entire relfector were designed correctly to face straight back.

All this was perhaps more detailed than you expected. But I have decided to present this much detail, so you are in a better position to understand the problems of nighttime cycling. The conclusion from all this reasoning can be summarized briefly: install a big bright white light in the front and at least a big flat reflector in the back, preferably amber (if permitted by your state's Vehicle Code). In addition, a bright rear light will also make you visible to bicyclists and others who ride without adequate headlights.

On mountain bikes, battery lighting is probably the most appropriate; generators would get damaged in off-road use. Perhaps the best battery lights are the British made Berec lights and optically similar models made by Cat-Eye. These units are powered by two D-cells, which last remarkably long if used with the proper bulb, namely twenty minutes each day for an entire month. Front and rear lights have been optically designed to project a very efficiently concentrated bundle of light on the road far ahead, and to be visible far to the back, respectively. Matching mounting hardware is available both for permanent installation and for easy removal. Amongst reflectors, your best choice by far is a standard highway marker reflector. Install lights as high as possible, so they are most readily visible to others and project onto the road under the most favorable angle. Reflectors should be mounted lower down, so they pick up a low beam.

The Pump

Don't set out without a pump on your bike, and take it with you when you leave the bike anywhere, so it doesn't get ripped off. Make sure the pump is designed to fit the kind of valves you use (my recommendation is to use tubes with Presta valves, as explained in chapter 16). The best pump I know is the French Zéfal, which has an air-tight closure to clamp around the valve.

For home use, you will find the hand pump a little tiring and may consider getting a larger-volume stand pump, operated either by hand or foot. The big pump should have a built-in pressure gauge. For on-the-road use, a separate pressure gauge for the appropriate type of valve is also recommended.

Water Bottle

Install at least one water bottle cage on the bicycle, more if you plan to be travelling further. The water bottle itself should have a pull-type closure,

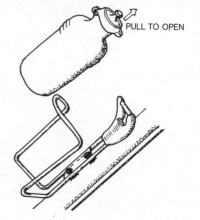
PULL TO OPEN

Take along these tools: screwdriver, tire irons, patch kit, Allen wrench, adjustable wrench and needle nose pliers. On a longer trip you'll need more tools. And never go without a pump.

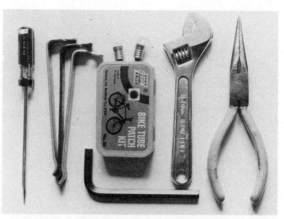

which can be operated conveniently while riding. The cheapest good water bottle I've ever seen was a shampoo bottle with a pivoting squirt top. I carry two water bottles: one filled with water, the other with fruit juice, providing quick nourishment on a long ride. The bottle cage should be attached to braze-ons, installed on the frame, because the mountain bike's thicker frame tubes don't accept most clamps.

Tools
You needn't be a travelling workshop, but having access to at least the most elementary tools on the bike is great for your peace of mind, and even greater when you do develop a problem away from home. Here is a list of things I carry on any trip close enough to civilization to limp into a store or a garage within a couple of hours:
– tire patch kit (check to make sure the patches are still there and the rubber solution is not dried up)
– three tire irons
– six-inch long adjustable wrench
– small screwdriver
– crank extractor tool
– 6 mm Allen wrench
– needle nose pliers

All these things held together in a little pouch with a rag and some waterless hand cleanser.

For longer trips, I recommend you assemble your personal tool kit with exactly those tools that are appropriate for your bike and its equipment. Spend an afternoon to establish just which tools and which sizes (and how many of each) you may need to carry out literally every repair on your bike. If you go about it carefully, you'll be astonished how little it takes to do that. And it's extremely rewarding. This kit should definitely include lubricants and some elementary spares (brake cables, spokes, bolts and nuts, inner tube, etc.).

And More?
There are dozens of gadgets on the market, and lots of people will buy them: electronic speedometers, pulse rate counters, rear view mirrors, safety flags, power horns... Don't let too many things like that come between you and your bicycle, because they can't do much except distract from the simple joys of riding your bike. The modern off-road bicycle is a delightful machine: uncomplicated and functional. Keep it that way.

Appendix

Table 1 – Gear table for 26-in wheels

Number of teeth on chainwheel

Number of teeth on sprocket	24	26	28	30	32	34	36	38	39	40	41	42	43	44	45	46	47	48	49	50	51	52	53	Number of teeth on sprocket
13	48	52	56	60	64	68	72	76	78	80	82	84	86	88	90	92	94	96	98	100	102	104	106	13
14	45	48	52	56	60	63	67	70	72	74	76	78	80	82	84	85	87	89	91	93	95	97	98	14
15	42	45	49	52	55	59	62	66	68	69	71	73	75	76	78	80	81	83	85	87	88	90	92	15
16	39	42	45	49	52	55	58	61	63	65	67	68	70	72	73	75	76	78	80	81	83	85	86	16
17	37	40	43	46	49	52	55	58	60	61	63	64	66	67	69	70	72	73	75	76	78	80	81	17
18	35	38	40	43	46	49	52	55	56	58	59	61	62	64	65	66	68	69	71	72	74	75	77	18
19	33	36	38	41	44	47	49	52	53	55	56	57	59	60	62	63	64	66	67	68	70	71	73	19
20	31	34	36	39	42	44	47	49	51	52	53	55	56	57	59	60	61	62	64	65	66	68	69	20
21	30	32	35	37	40	42	45	47	48	50	51	52	53	54	56	57	58	59	61	62	63	64	66	21
22	28	31	33	35	38	40	43	45	46	47	48	50	51	52	53	54	56	57	58	59	60	61	63	22
23	27	29	32	34	36	38	41	43	44	45	46	47	49	50	51	52	53	54	55	57	58	59	60	23
24	26	28	30	32	35	37	39	41	42	43	44	45	47	48	49	50	51	52	53	54	55	56	57	24
25	25	27	29	31	33	35	37	39	41	42	43	44	45	46	47	48	49	50	51	52	53	54	55	25
26	24	26	28	30	32	34	36	38	39	40	41	42	43	44	45	46	47	48	49	50	51	52	53	26
27	23	25	27	29	31	33	35	37	38	39	39	40	41	42	43	44	45	46	47	48	49	50	51	27
28	22	24	26	28	30	32	33	35	36	37	38	39	40	41	42	43	44	45	46	46	47	48	49	28
30	21	23	24	26	28	29	31	33	34	35	36	36	37	38	39	40	41	42	42	43	44	45	46	30
32	20	21	23	24	26	28	29	31	32	33	33	34	35	36	37	37	38	39	40	41	41	42	43	32
34	18	20	21	23	24	26	28	29	30	31	31	32	33	33	34	35	36	37	37	38	39	40	41	34
38	16	18	19	21	22	23	25	26	27	27	28	29	29	30	31	31	32	33	34	34	35	36	36	38
Number of teeth on sprocket	24	26	28	30	32	34	36	38	39	40	41	42	43	44	45	46	47	48	49	50	51	52	53	

Refer to chapters 5 and 15 for explanation

Table 2 – Troubleshooting guide

Problem/symptom	Possible cause	Required correction	For description see
bike hard to ride (high resistance when coasting and pedalling)	1. insufficient tire pressure	inflate and/or mend tire (use high-pressure pump)	chapter 16 (tires) chapter 18 (pump)
	2. wheel rubs on brake, fork or frame	adjust brake; adjust or straighten wheel; install narrower tire if insufficient clearance	chapter 16 (wheel) chapter 17 (brake)
	3. dirt build-up on wheel or bike	clean bike	chapter 2
	4. resistance in wheel bearings	lubricate, adjust or overhaul wheel bearings	chapter 16
bike hard to pedal (but coasts alright)	1. accumulated dirt on chain	clean chain, chainwheels, sprockets and derailleurs	chapters 2, 14, 15
	2. insufficient lubrication on chain	lubricate	chapter 14
	3. resistance in bottom bracket or pedal bearings	lubricate, adjust or overhaul bearings	chapter 14
chain drops off chain-wheel or sprocket	1. derailleur out of adjustment	adjust derailleurs	chapter 15
gears do not engage properly	1. shift lever dirty, loose or defective	clean, adjust, lubricate or replace	chapters 2 and 15
	2. derailleur cable anchor or guides loose, or cable corroded	tighten attachments or replace cable	chapter 15
	3. derailleur out of adjustment	adjust derailleur	chapter 15
	4. chain too short or too long	correct or replace	chapter 14

Problem	Cause	Remedy	Reference
inadequate braking	1. rim or brake wet, greasy or dirty	clean rim and brake	chapters 2, 16, 17
	2. brakes out of adjustment	adjust brakes	chapter 17
	3. friction in brake cables	replace or lubricate	chapter 17
	4. brake shoe worn	replace brake shoe	chapter 17
brakes squeak	1. brake attachment loose	adjust and tighten	chapter 17
	2. brake pad worn	replace	chapter 17
	3. rim or brake pad dirty	clean or replace pad	chapters 2 and 17
	(if none of these causes: don't worry, some brakes just squeak)		
chain slips	1. chain and sprockets dirty	clean and lubricate	chapters 2 and 14
	2. rear derailleur out of adjustment	adjust	chapter 15
	3. chain worn (especially when used with new freewheel)	replace chain	chapter 14
	4. freewheel sprocket worn	replace sprocket or freewheel	chapter 14
irregular pedalling movement	1. crank or pedal loose	tighten cranks and pedals	chapter 14
	2. pedal or bottom bracket bearing out of adjustment	adjust or overhaul	chapter 14
	3. crank, chainwheel or pedal axle bent	replace or get straightened	chapter 14 / bike mechanic
steering vibrates or is inprecise	1. wheels out of true or not in line	center and true both wheels and, if necessary, get frame and fork aligned	chapter 16 / bike mechanic
	2. head-set bearings loose or worn	adjust, overhaul or replace	chapter 12
	3. wheel bearings loose	adjust or overhaul	chapter 16

Further Reading

To date there is not much literature written specifically for the mountain bike rider. However, quite a bit of information can be obtained by careful study of the regular bicycling press. One magazine, *The Fat-Tire Flyer,* addresses itself exclusively to off-road cycling enthusiasts. Other magazines, such as *Bicycling, Bicycle Guide, American Bicyclist, American Bicyclist and Motorcyclist,* and *California Bicyclist,* frequently contain articles dealing with both equipment and techniques of interest to the mountain bike rider. The addresses of these periodicals may be found below under *Useful Addresses.*

Much of the information the mountain bike owner seeks may be found in general bicycle publications. These include the magazines mentioned above, as well as an impressive number of books. Here follows a brief description of the books which I consider most useful.

John Forester, *Effective Cycling.* MIT-Press, Cambridge, 1984.
Not the prettiest, nor even the easiest to read, but far and away the most authoritative manual on how to ride sanely and safely. Forester's emphasis is on cycling on regular roads, making equipment recommendations to match. Just the same, it is an excellent source of all sorts of informtion important to off-road cycling as well.

Fred DeLong, *DeLong's Guide to Bicycles and Bicycling.* Chilton Books, Radnor, 1984.
This is by far the most complete and thorough treatment of the mechanical aspects of the bicycle and its equipment. DeLong and I don't always see eye to eye when it comes to safety-related issues (I shall not deny being more partial to John Forester's approach), but his treatment of equipment-related material is superb.

Raymond Bridge, *Bike Touring, The Sierra Club Guide to Outings on Wheels.* Sierra Club Books, San Francisco, 1979.
The best of the many books devoted to bicycle touring. Written for folks with skinny tires at a time when there was nothing else, it is still an equally good source in the age of fat tires.

John Allen, *The Complete Book of Bike Commuting.* Rodale Press, Emmaus, 1981.
A thorough and well-illustrated guide for any kind of urban cycling, whether to work or not. Allen's recommendations for riding in traffic should be framed and hung on every cyclist's wall.

C.W. Coles and H.T. Glenn, *Glenn's Complete Bicycle Manual.* Crown Publishers, New York, 1973.
Forget the 'complete' in the title: it's only one thing, namely a very thorough repair manual. All other information in the book is useless, but as a repair manual it is superb.

F.R. Whitt and D.G. Wilson, *Bicycling Science.* MIT-Press, Cambridge, 1982.
If you want to know a lot about bicycles, their history, their development and their possibilities, and if you can stomach graphs and formulas, you will find this a fascinating source.

I.E. Faria and P.R. Cavanagh, *The Physiology and Biomechanics of Cycling.* Wiley, New York, 1978.
Less complicated and more practical than the title suggests, this is a nice little book. It tells the cyclist a lot about his performance and that of his bicycle.

J. Krausz and V. Van der Reis-Krausz, *The Bicycling Book.* Dial Press, New York, 1982.
If you're in love with your bike, there's so much interesting stuff here that you can spend years leafing through this book and reading what turns you on. Even if you weren't in love with your bike before, you'll probably be once you have read this book.

Rob Van der Plas, *The Penguin Bicycle Handbook.* Penguin Books, London and New York, 1983.
Forgive me for pushing my own book, but in all modesty, it's considered the best small paperback amongst the general bicycle books. The book was written for the British market, but once you get used to some of the peculiarities of the language as it is spoken in that neck of the woods, you'll find this a very comprehensive source of general and technical information.

Rob Van der Plas, *The Bicycle Repair Book.* Bicycle Books, San Francisco, 1985.
Written to satisfy the needs of anyone who will ever be confronted with the need to repair or maintain a bicycle. A very systematic approach, with step-by-step instructions and trouble-shooting tables, probably make this the most practical repair guide on the market.

Archibald Sharp, *Bicycles and Tricycles, an Elementary Treatise on Their Design and Construction.* MIT-Press, Cambridge, 1977.
Not your everyday book, but a fascinating source for anybody interested in the engineering design principles of the bicycle. This book, which was briefly mentioned in chapter 10, is a fascimile reprint of the original which appeared in 1896. Nearly a century later it is still the best, if not the only, book of its kind.

Useful Addresses

Organizations

NORBA (National Off-Road Bicycling Association), 2175 Holly Lane, Solvang, CA 93463.

The Rough Stuff Fellowship, c/o A. John Mathews, 9 Liverpool Avenue, Southport, Lancashire PR8 3NE (Great Britain).

Bicycle USA (League of American Wheelmen), P.O.Box 988, Baltimore, MD 21203.

CTC (Cyclists' Touring Club), 69 Meadrow, Godalming, Surrey GU7 3HS (Great Britain)

Bikecentennial, P.O.Box 8308, Missoula, MT 59807.

Suppliers and Organizers

To avoid favoring some suppliers, manufacturers or organizers at the expense of others, I do not provide the addresses of individual businesses. Good sources of such information are the various bicycle periodicals, as well as the following publication:

Nicholas Crane (Ed.), International Cycling Guide (annual), New York, Zoetrope.

Periodicals

The Fat-Tire Flyer, P.O.Box 757, Fairfax, CA 94930.

Bicycling, 33 E. Minor Street, Emmaus, PA 18049 (also publishes Bike-Tech).

Bicycle Guide, 128 N 11th Street, Allentown, PA 18102.

Bicycle Sport, P.O.Box 5277, Torrance, CA 90510.

American Bicyclist and Motorcyclist, 461 – 8th Avenue, New York, NY 10001.

California Bicyclist, P.O. Box 210477, San Francisco, CA 94121.

Bicycle, 89-91 Bayham Street, London NW1 OAG (Great Britain).

Bicycle Times, 26 Commercial Bldgs., Dunston, Tyne and Wear, NE 11 9AA (Great Britain).

Cycletouring (CTC-members' magazine, Great Britain – for address see Organizations).

American Bicyclist (Bicycle USA-members' magazine – for address see Organizations).

Great Expeditions, Box 46499, Station G, Vancouver, BC V6R 4G7 (Canada).

Index